Fourmile Canyon Fire Findings

Russell Graham, Mark Finney, Chuck McHugh, Jack Cohen, Dave Calkin,
Rick Stratton, Larry Bradshaw, Ned Nikolov

I0434789

United States Department of Agriculture / Forest Service

Rocky Mountain Research Station

General Technical Report RMRS-GTR-289

August 2012

Abstract

The Fourmile Canyon Fire burned in the fall of 2010 in the Rocky Mountain Front Range adjacent to Boulder, Colorado. The fire occurred in steep, rugged terrain, primarily on privately owned mixed ponderosa pine and Douglas-fir forests. The fire started on September 6 when the humidity of the air was very dry ($\approx$ <7%) and the winds were steadily blowing in the range of 15 miles per hour and gusting to over 40 miles per hour. These conditions prevailed for most of the first day when the fire burned approximately 5,700 acres and destroyed 162 homes. Because of the windy conditions, aircraft could not be used until late that first day. The first responders concentrated on evacuating the occupants of the 474 homes in the fire vicinity. No public or firefighters were injured during the course of the fire. This outcome was directly related to the excellent preparedness of Boulder County and, in particular, the Sheriff's Department and the local fire districts. Fuel treatments had previously been applied to several areas within the fire perimeter to modify fire behavior and/or burn severity if a wildfire was to occur. However, the fuel treatments had minimal impact in affecting how the fire burned or the damage it caused. After the initial day of intense burning and 4 additional days of relatively benign fire behavior, the Fourmile Canyon Fire had burned 6,181 acres and become one of the most damaging fires in Colorado's history. This report summarizes how the fire burned, the damage it caused, and offers insights to help the residents and first responders prepare for the next wildfire that will burn on the Colorado Front Range.

Fourmile Canyon Fire Assessment Team:

Russ Graham, Assessment team leader: Research Forester, U.S. Forest Service, Rocky Mountain Research Station, Moscow, Idaho.

Mark Finney, Fire behavior assessment: Research Forester, U.S. Forest Service Rocky Mountain Research Station, Missoula, Montana.

Chuck McHugh, Fire behavior assessment: Fire Spatial Analyst, U.S. Forest Service Rocky Mountain Research Station, Missoula, Montana.

Jack Cohen, Home destruction assessment: Research Physical Scientist, U.S. Forest Service Rocky Mountain Research Station, Missoula, Montana.

Dave Calkin, Economics/Social assessment: Research Forester, U.S. Forest Service Rocky Mountain Research Station, Missoula, Montana.

Rick Stratton, Home destruction assessment: Fire Analyst, U.S. Forest Service Pacific Northwest Region, Portland, Oregon.

Larry Bradshaw, Fire weather assessment: Meteorologist, U.S. Forest Service Rocky Mountain Research Station, Missoula, Montana.

Ned Nikolov, Fire weather assessment: Air Resource Specialist, U.S. Forest Service Rocky Mountain Research Station, Fort Collins, Colorado.

Contents

Introduction 1

Methods 6

    Data Collection 6

Physical Setting 7

Infrastructure 11

Pre-Fire 15

    Antecedent Weather and Fire Danger 16
    Winds 20
    Fuel Treatments 21

Fourmile Canyon Fire 29

    Fire Weather 29
    Initial Response 33

Fire Behavior 35

Fire Suppression 42

    September 6 43
    September 7 47
    September 8 48
    September 9 49
    September 10 51
    September 11 52
    September 12 52
    September 13-17 52

Aerial Resources 52

Fuel Treatment Efficacy 55

Home Destruction 60

    Residential Wildfire Results 60
    Home Destruction 64
    Key Elements for Preventing WUI Fire Disasters 69

Social/Economic.. **69**

    Fire Management Costs 69
    Economic Losses 73
    Social Attitudes 73
    Fuel Treatment Costs 74

Strategic Wildfire Risk Management **75**

    Fire Prevention 76
    Incident Response.. 76
    Fuels Management 77
    Home Ignition Zone 77

Summary **78**

    Weather.. 78
    Fire Behavior 79
    Fuel Treatments... 79
    Suppression... 80
    Home Destruction 80
    Social/Economics 81

Acknowledgments... **81**

References **82**

Appendix A: Senator Udall's Letter **85**

Appendix B: Response to Manager Comments Received on
    Preliminary Draft... **86**

    U.S. Forest Service, Rocky Mountain Region (Region-2) 86
    Colorado State Forest Service Comments... 99
    Bureau Land Management Comments... 104

Apendix C: Summary of Contacted Individuals **108**

Fourmile Canyon Fire Findings

Russell Graham, Mark Finney, Chuck McHugh, Jack Cohen,
Dave Calkin, Rick Stratton, Larry Bradshaw, Ned Nikolov

Introduction

Wildfires are a common occurrence on the Front Range Mountains of Colorado. The historical mean fire return interval in low elevation ponderosa pine (*Pinus ponderosa*) forests in the northern Colorado Front Range varies from 8 to 18 years (Veblen and others 2000). Even though current fires are aggressively suppressed, many large fires have burned along the Front Range in the past 30 years as exemplified by the Black Tiger Fire in 1989 and the Hayman Fire in 2002 (Figures 1, 2) (Graham 2003, NFPA 1989). During the period from 1980 through 2011, 48 fires burned 242,457 acres along the Front Range; 13 of these fires blackened 205,148 of the total acres and destroyed 476 homes (Figure 2). Every 2 years on average, somewhere in the Colorado Front Range a wildfire burns, impacting a significant number of structures (Table 1). Within Boulder County, large fires involving home loss account for only 8.6 percent of the total area burned along the Colorado Front Range but 49.6 percent of the homes lost (Table 1). These large fires can occur any time of the year and typically burn when the wind speeds are high and the air is dry. During these conditions, which are very common on the Front Range, fire suppression efforts are typically ineffective and fires readily escape initial attack (Stephens and Ruth 2005).

The weather for summer of 2010 along the Front Range was not abnormal. However, August had above normal temperatures and below normal rain fall and by September the area was in a short-term drought. The fine dead fuels in the ponderosa pine/juniper (*Juniperus* spp.) and Douglas-fir (*Pseudotsuga menziesii*)/ponderosa pine forests west of Boulder, Colorado, were dry. Live fuel (e.g., trees, grasses, shrubs) moistures were at or just below normal for the time of year. Leaf fall and curing of grasses were following their normal patterns and no vegetative killing frost had occurred by the time of the fire. Downslope winds, common in early September along the Front Range, were blowing steadily in the range of 10 to 15 miles per hour with gusts increasing from 24 to 41 miles per hour between 0700 and 1000 the morning of September 6. At 1002 an emergency 911 call reported a fire burning in the lower portion of Emerson Gulch near where it intersects with Fourmile Canyon Drive. Within 6 miles of Boulder, the Fourmile Canyon Fire destroyed more homes than any other wildfire in Colorado's history (Figure 3).

Being located near Boulder, the area where the fire burned contained many homes, businesses, and recreational lands. Because of these values and the 3,500 residents evacuated from the area, the fire was the nation's top fire priority at the time. Even though the Fourmile Canyon Fire occurred during different months and synoptic weather patterns than the Black Tiger and Hayman Fires, the weather, fuels, and topography combined to create similar fire spread conditions as they each escaped aggressive initial attack. Understanding how this fire burned, the damage it caused, and how people and agencies respond to such emergencies can reinforce the conclusions of the Black Tiger Fire Case Study (NFPA 1989) and the Hayman Fire Case Study (Graham 2003) and will help prepare for the next wildfire on the Front Range.

USDA Forest Service Gen. Tech. Rep. RMRS-GTR-289. 2012

1

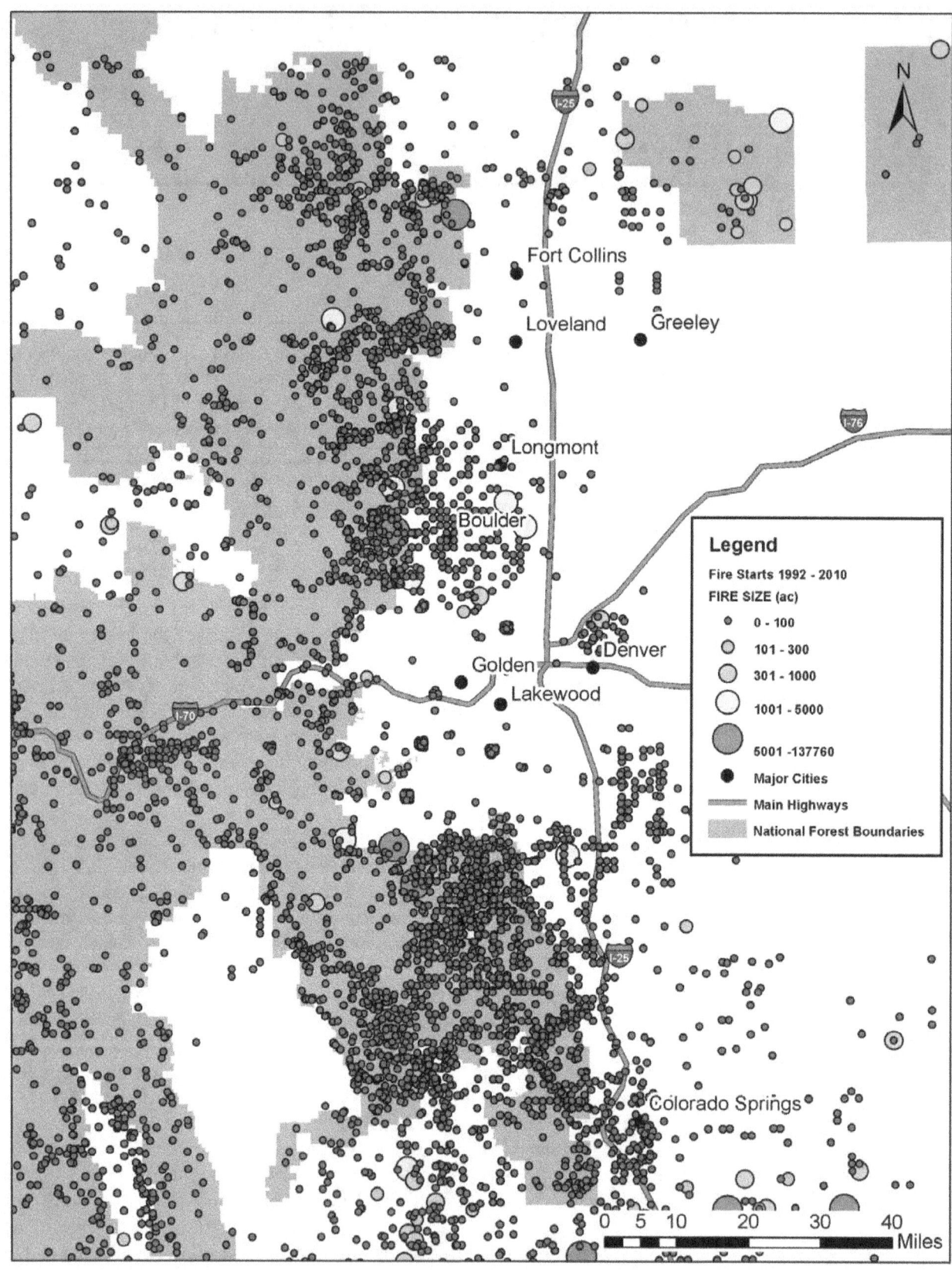

Figure 1. Wildfire occurrence on the Colorado Front Range from 1992 to 2009 expressed as fire start locations by final fire size (see Figure 2).

USDA Forest Service Gen. Tech. Rep. RMRS-GTR-289. 2012

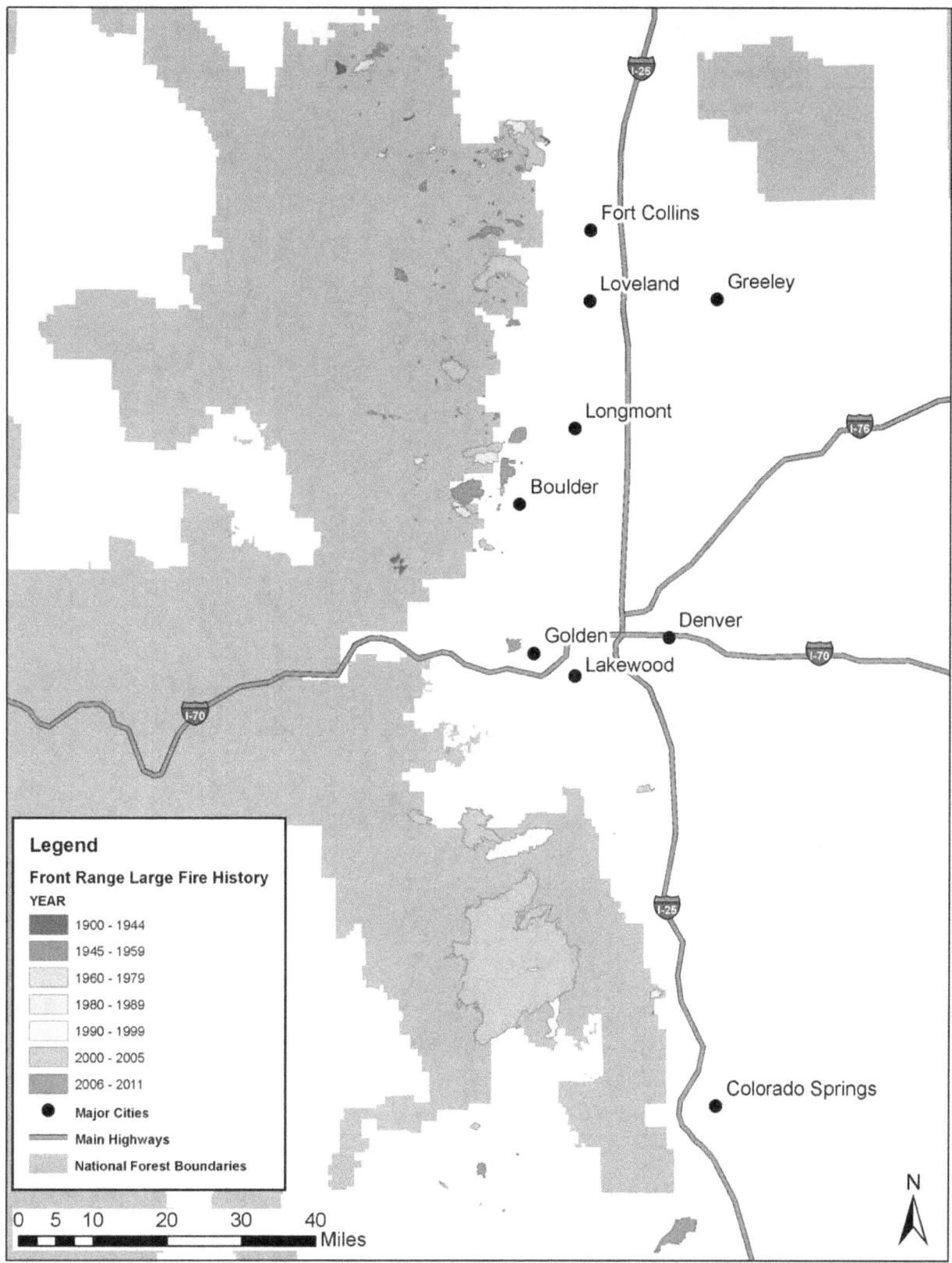

Figure 2. Burned areas of fires by time period. Note that the completeness of spatial fire records is not consistent among agencies responsible for fire suppression and reporting (e.g. federal, state, county etc.); non-federal lands tend to show fewer fires because state and county geospatial records are not available (see Figure 1).

USDA Forest Service Gen. Tech. Rep. RMRS-GTR-289. 2012

3

Table 1. Major wildfires that burned on federal, state and private lands throughout Colorado between 1976 and 2011. Original Source: http://csfs.colostate.edu/pages/wf-historical-facts.html. Additional fires were added by the review team.

Year	Month[a]	Fire name	Cause[b]	Size (acres)	No. homes destroyed	Fatalities[c]
1976	July	Battlement Mesa	L	880	0	3
1978	September	Murphy Gulch	H	3,300	1 unoccupied home	0
1989	July	Black Tigerd	H	1,778	44 homes	0
1990	November	Olde Stage [d]	H	3,000	10 homes	0
1994	July	South Canyon	L	2,115	0	14
1994	July	Hourglass Fire	L	1,275	13 buildings	0
1996	May	Buffalo Creek [e]	H	12,000	10 homes	0
1999	June	Battlement Mesa	H	156	9 homes	0
2000	June	Hi Meadow [e]	H	10,800	51 homes	0
2000	June	Bobcat [e]	H	10,599	18 homes	0
2000	July	Bircher (Mesa Verde)	L	19,709	0	0
2001	October	Carter Lake/Armageddon	H	1,216	0	0
2002	April	Snaking [e]	H	2,590	0	0
2002	April	Cuerno Verde	H	388	2 homes	2
2002	May	Schoonover [e]	L	3,860	13 structures	0
2002	June	Trinidad Complex	L	32,896	0	0
2002	June	Iron Mountain	H	4,400	100+ cabins, etc	0
2002	June	Coal Seam	Coal Seam	12,209	29 homes	0
2002	June	Hayman [e]	H	137,760	133 homes	5
2002	June	Missionary Ridge	H	70,485	56 homes	1
2002	June	Miracle Complex	L	3,951	0	0
2002	June	Million	H	9,346	11 homes	0
2002	August	Mt. Zirkel Complex	L	31,016	0	0
2002	July	Big Elk [e]	H	4,413	0	3
2002	July	Big Fish	L	17,056	lodge + 7 cabins	0
2002	July	Long Mesa	L	2,601	3 homes	0
2002	July	Panorama	H	1,700	4 homes	0
2003	July	Brush Mountain	H	5,292	0	0
2003	October	Overland [d]	H	3,439	12 homes	0
2003	October	Cherokee Ranch	H	1,200	2 homes	0
2004	March	Picnic Rock [e]	H	8,908	1 home	0
2005	July	Mason	L	11,357	0	0
2006	January	Mauricio Canyon	H	3,825	0	0
2006	March	Yuma County	Power Lines	23,000	0	0
2006	June	Thomas	L	3,347	0	0
2006	June	Mato Vega	L	13,820	0	0
2009	January	Old Stage [d]	Power Lines	3,169	1 home	0
2010	September	Fourmile Canyon [d]	H	6,181	168 homes	0
2010	September	Reservoir Road [e]	H	754	2 homes	0
2011	April	Crystal [e]	H	2,940	13 homes	0

[a] Month of fire origin.
[b] Cause: L(Lightning); H(Human).
[c] All fatalities listed in this table are firefighters, air tanker, and helicopter pilots. Fatalities for the Hayman Fire are the result of an auto accident while en-route to the fire.
[d] Fires located within Boulder County and along the Front Range of Colorado 1976-2011.
[e] Fires located along the Front Range of Colorado 1976-2011.

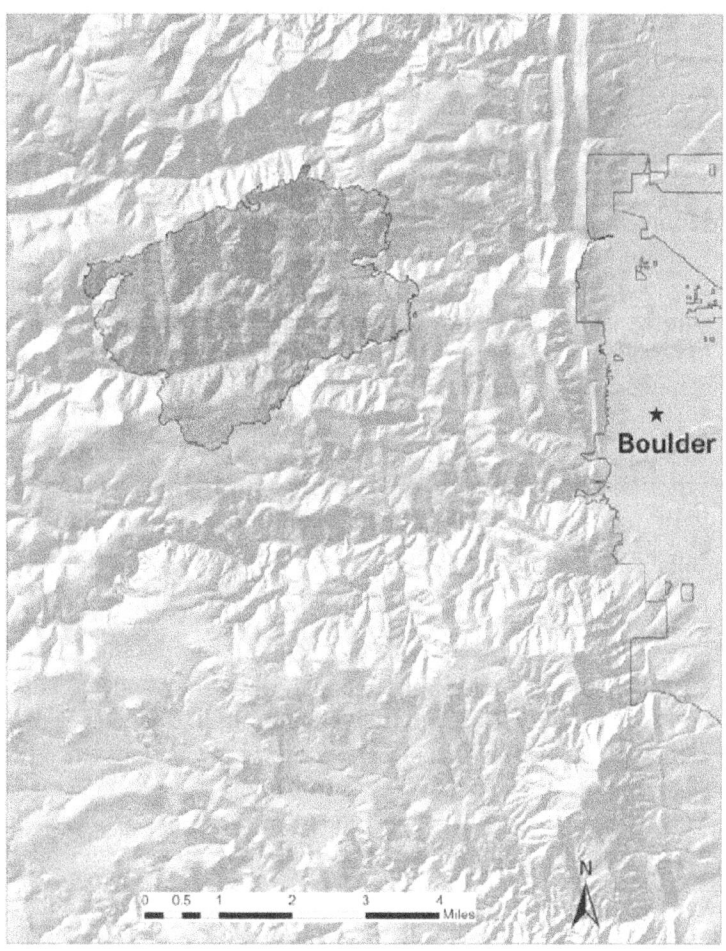

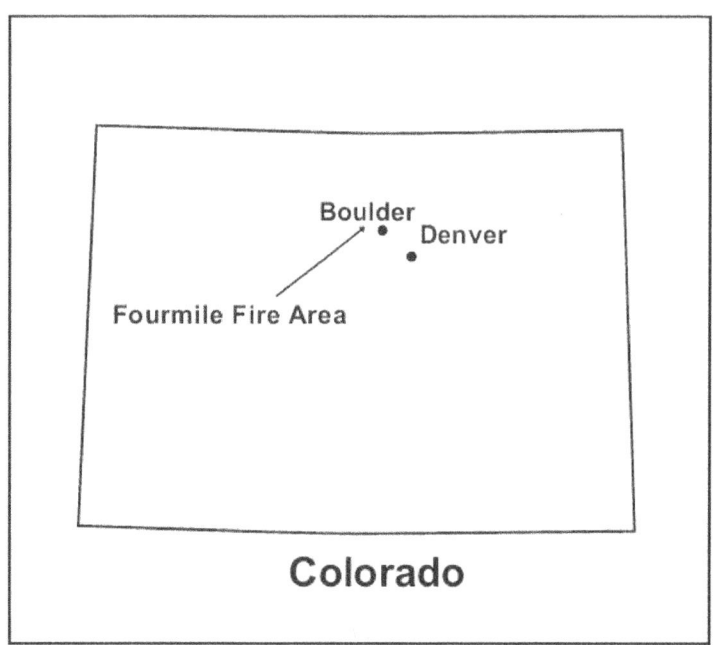

Figure 3. Location of the Fourmile Canyon Fire that burned along the foothills west of Boulder, Colorado, on September 6 through 17, 2010.

USDA Forest Service Gen. Tech. Rep. RMRS-GTR-289. 2012

5

As such, Senator Mark Udall suggested to Secretary of Agriculture Vilsack and Governor Ritter, that the U.S. Forest Service and the Colorado State Forest Service review the fire to explore these issues as to inform future decisions (Appendix A). The Forest Service, Rocky Mountain Region, in collaboration with the Forest Service, Rocky Mountain Research Station and the Colorado State Forest Service, agreed to assess the Fourmile Canyon Fire. In accordance with the Federal Advisory Committee Act (FACA), the Rocky Mountain Research Station assembled a team to assess the fire. Being a review of the Fourmile Canyon Fire, this assessment does not, nor was it intended to be a literature review of wildfire behavior, suppression, fuel treatments, or other subjects germane to wildfires. We include relevant references in this assessment and we direct the reader to those documents and the literature cited in them for further discussions on fuels, fire behavior, and allied subjects.

Methods

In developing our assessment, we did our best to address the questions raised by Senator Udall (Appendix A). We gathered abundant air tanker data because air tanker use was a major concern during the fire. Due to limited resources, the Assessment Team made minimal visits to the Fourmile Canyon Fire during and immediately after the fire. However, meteorological, remotely sensed, and geospatial data were readily available post-fire and became an important part of the data collected by the Team. A key limitation to these types of reviews is that very little firsthand knowledge of the fire can be gathered, so post-fire forensic, interviews, and remotely sensed data dominate. By March 2011, the Team was able to begin in earnest gathering data, which, compared to other fires we have assessed, were abundant. We not only gathered data but we filtered it for relevance and validity. Team visits to the fire area equaled a total of ≈70 person days.

Data Collection

Our data collection included, but was not limited to:

- On site, telephone, letter, and e-mail interviews
    - Colorado State Forest Service
    - U.S. Forest Service
    - Bureau of Land Management
    - Fire Protection Districts
    - Boulder County Parks and Open Space
    - Boulder County Sheriff's Department
    - Boulder County Fourmile Canyon Fire Recovery staff
    - Boulder County Assessor's Office
    - Incident Management Teams
    - Firefighters
    - Rocky Mountain Insurance Information Association
- Remote sensing geospatial information
    - Color infrared satellite imagery
    - Burn severity mapping
    - Photography
    - Home locations
- Media: pictures and videos
    - Denver television
    - Denver news papers
- Law-enforcement and fire department dispatch transcripts
- Boulder County Assessor's Office
    - Valuation
    - Home loss

Physical Setting_____

The Fourmile Canyon Fire burned along the northern Front Range of the Rocky Mountains approximately 6 miles west of Boulder, Colorado (Figure 3). The fire burned in an area with rugged and complex topography with elevations ranging from 5,361 to 9,348 feet (Figure 4). Prominent topographic features in the area include: Emancipation Hill, Monument Hill, Bald Mountain, Sugarloaf Mountain, Big Horn Point, and Big Horn Mountain. Fourmile Creek and Gold Run Creek are major drainages within the fire area. Fourmile Creek runs west to east and then turns to the southeast as Gold Run Creek enters from the northwest (Figure 4). Narrow (≈<100 ft) riparian areas are typical along many of the streams. These primary and other drainages in the area contain many steep side slopes with some exceeding 98 percent or nearly 45 degrees. All (i.e., north, east, west, south) slope aspects are represented in the area where the fire burned. However, long expanses of steep southerly slopes are frequent.

For the most part, the soils in the area are derived from metamorphic and igneous rocks. Along with the steep side slopes, many rock outcrops and granitic intrusions occur in the area. These and other parent materials in the area give rise to coarse textured and sandy soils that are poorly developed, shallow, and well drained (USDA-NRCS 2008).

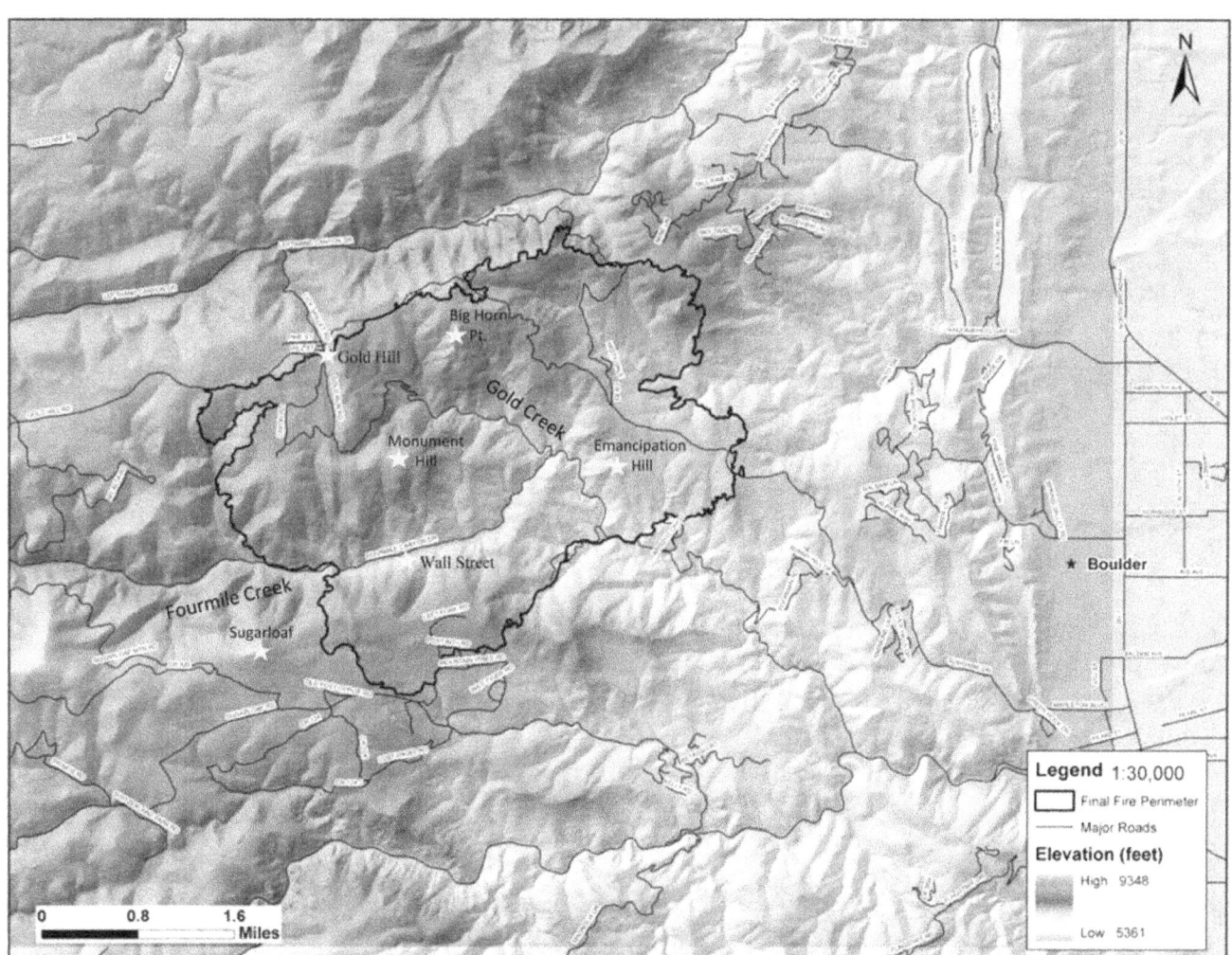

Figure 4. Topography where the Fourmile Canyon Fire burned is very rugged with steep slopes and narrow canyons. Fourmile and Gold Creek are the primary drainages in the area.

USDA Forest Service Gen. Tech. Rep. RMRS-GTR-289. 2012

7

A continental climate typifies the area where the fire burned. An average of 18.7 inches of precipitation falls each year and the mean annual temperature is 51.3 °F with a mean annual summer temperature of 70.1 °F (Boulder Station 050848, 1893-2010, Western Regional Climate Center, http://www.wrcc.dri.edu/cgi-bin/cliMAIN.pl?co0848). Precipitation occurs primarily during the winter and spring, with the peak precipitation occurring during April and May. Weather patterns during the fire season along the Front Range of Colorado are often punctuated by warm (≈80 °F), dry (≈<20% relative humidity), and strong (20 + mph) winds (Cohen 1976).

Vegetation in the area where the fire burned is typical for the montane zone of the Colorado Front Range, and varies with elevation. The south-facing slopes in the lower montane zone (5,900 to 7,700 feet) are usually covered by open park-like stands of ponderosa pine, often mixed with Rocky Mountain juniper (*Juniperus scopulorum*). Depending on soil conditions, abundant grasses and forbs along with common juniper (*Juniperus communis)* and mountain mahogany (*Cercocarpus* spp.) shrubs typify the ground-level vegetation (Figures 5-7). The north-facing aspects, which are usually moister than the southerly facing aspects, support mixed stands of ponderosa pine and Douglas-fir. Similar to the south-facing slopes, a rich understory of common juniper, mountain mahogany, and grasses often prevail (Figure 8). Cheatgrass (*Bromus tectorum*), a non-native species that is very flammable when dry, is the second most common grass in the area (Sherriff and Veblen 2007, 2008, Krasnow and others 2009, Keith and others 2010).

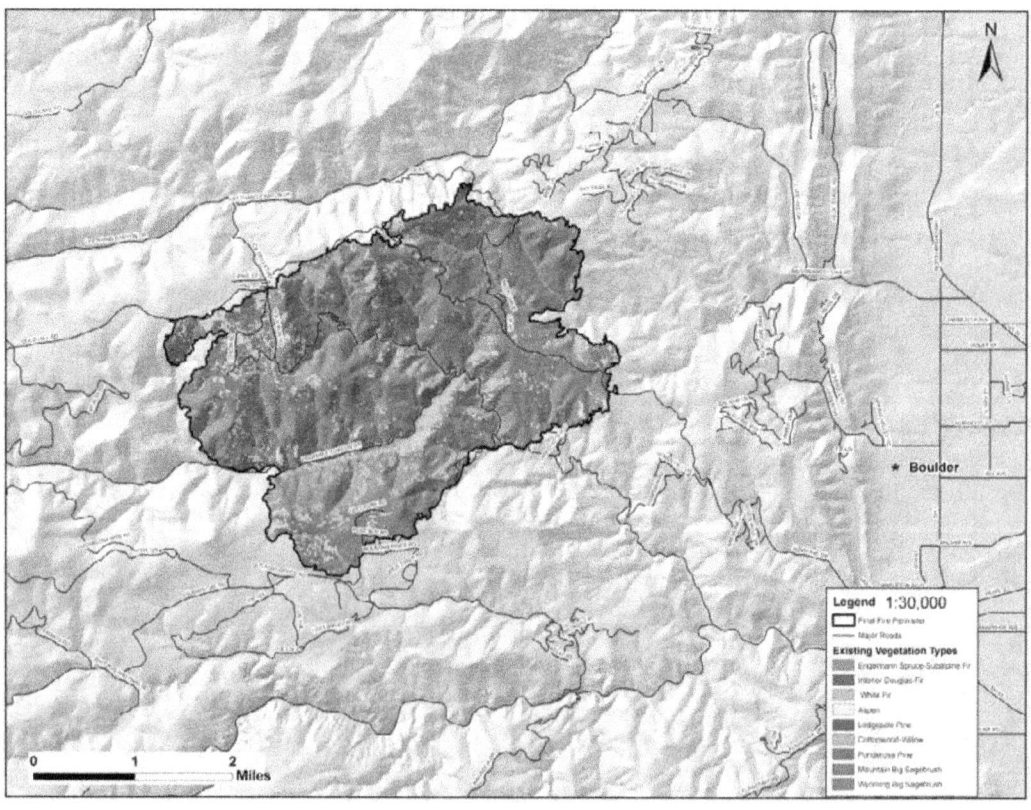

Figure 5. Vegetation where the Fourmile Canyon Fire burned is dominated by interior Douglas-fir/ponderosa pine forests on the south facing slopes and Douglas-fir forests on the north facing slopes (LANDFIRE 2010).

Figure 6. Typical open ponderosa pine forest occurring on the Front Range where the prairie transitions to the forest (photos: Russ Graham).

USDA Forest Service Gen. Tech. Rep. RMRS-GTR-289. 2012

9

Figure 7. A mixture of shrubs and grasses dominated the ground-level vegetation where the fire burned. Litter and downed woody material was continuous beneath forested areas (photos: Mike Tombolato (top); Russ Graham (bottom)).

Figure 8. Typical north facing slope occupied by a mixed Douglas-fir and ponderosa pine forest. Note the relatively closed canopy conditions of these forests compared to the open conditions of the ponderosa pine forests (see Figure 7) (photo: Russ Graham).

In the upper montane zone (7,700 to 9,350 feet), relatively dense and mixed stands of Douglas-fir and ponderosa pine usually dominate the north-facing slopes with a rich understory of grasses, forbs, and common juniper at ground-level. Open stands of ponderosa pine occupy the south-facing slopes with an abundant understory of shrubs and grasses, depending on soil conditions (Figures 5, 8) (Sherriff and Veblen 2007, 2008, Krasnow and others 2009). A review of Aerial Detection Survey (ADS) records obtained from Forest Health Protection indicates mountain pine beetles (*Dendroctonus ponderosae*) had been active within the final fire perimeter, attacking small patches of both lodgepole pine (*Pinus contorta*) and ponderosa pine. However, unlike other areas of Colorado, the area where the Fourmile Canyon Fire burned had no large expanses of beetle attacked or killed trees.

Infrastructure

Settlement began in the Fourmile Canyon Fire area in 1859 after gold was discovered. In 1860 a major wildfire burned in the area and the initial gold discoveries dwindled. As a result, the number of residents in the area decreased. In 1872 a rich form of tellurium (combination of gold and telluride minerals) was discovered and once again Gold Hill, Wall Street, and other communities in the area prospered (Figures 4, 9).

Figure 9. Wall Street and Gold Hill are two of the historic communities located in the area where the fire burned. Both were established in 1859 (photos: Russ Graham (top); Dave Steinmann (bottom)).

Mining claims dotted the area and roads connected the mining areas with the processing plants located along Fourmile Creek. A network of steep and narrow roads initially designed for use by wagons and pack trains dissects the area (Figure 10). The Lick Skillet Road offers access to Gold Hill from the north and is one of the steepest county roads in the United States. The mining legacy has led to a complex and linear land ownership pattern in the area, with private, Bureau of Land Management, Boulder County, U.S. Forest Service, and Colorado State Lands intermixed (Jessen 2011) (Figure 11).

Figure 10. Steep and narrow roads initially developed by the mining industry now provide access to the many homes (Melvina Road (top) and Emerson Gulch Road (bottom)) (photos: Russ Graham).

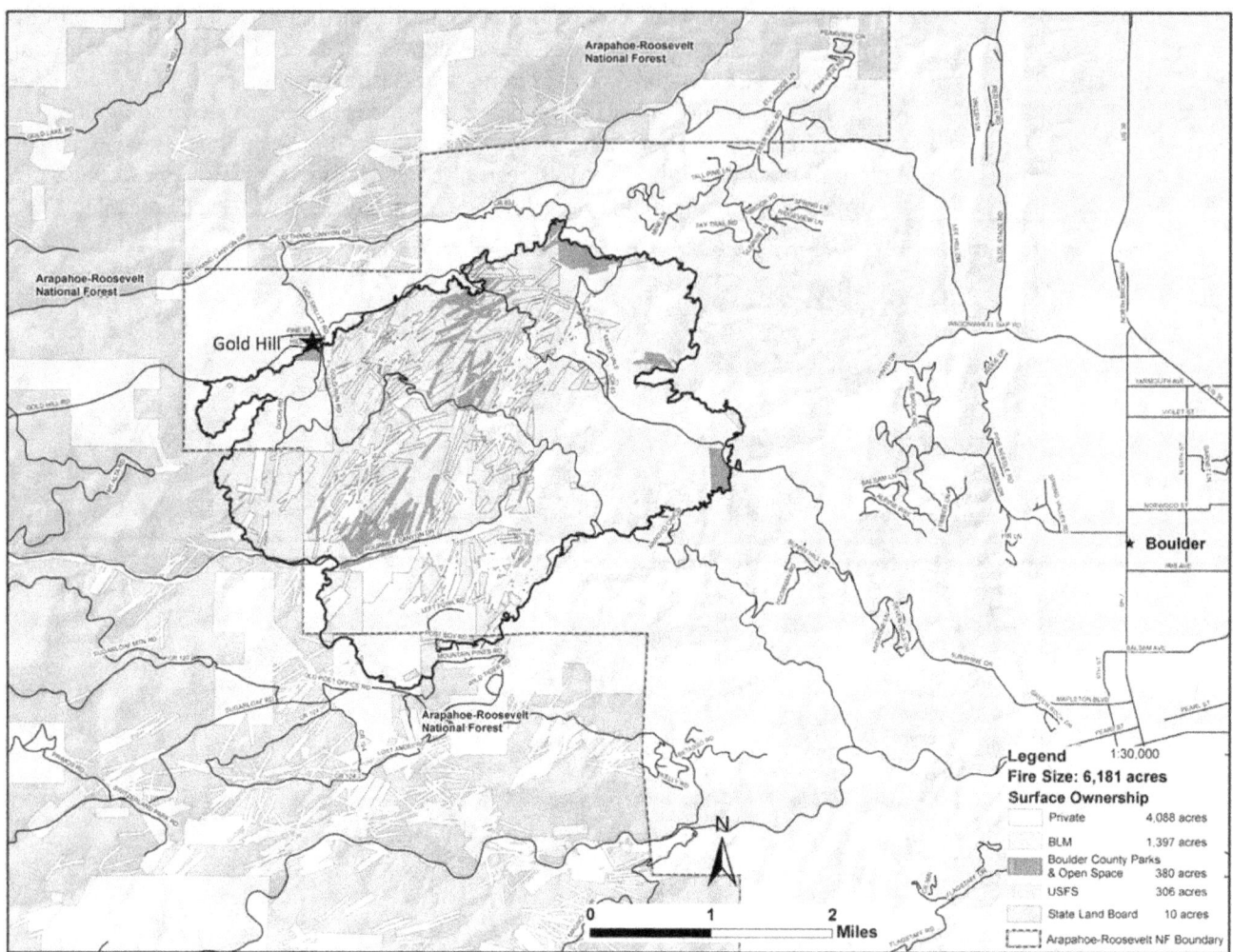

Figure 11. Land ownership within the Fourmile Canyon Fire is very complex as the result of mining. The Lick Skillet Road to Gold Hill from the north is one of the steepest county roads in the United States.

We identified 474 homes located within and adjacent (≈<100 feet) to the final fire perimeter. These homes are protected by the Fourmile, Sunshine, Sugar Loaf, and Gold Hill Fire Protection Districts (Figures 12, 13). Many homes were located on ridge tops, typified by those along Sunshine Canyon Drive, situated in the easterly portion of the area where the fire burned and along Fourmile and Gold Run Creeks. Gold Hill, located on the northern perimeter of the fire, and Wall Street, located along Fourmile Creek, are two of the historic communities located in the area. A combination of gravel and paved roads such as the Fourmile Canyon and Gold Run Roads, along with Sunshine Canyon Drive provide access to the area (Figure 12).

USDA Forest Service Gen. Tech. Rep. RMRS-GTR-289. 2012

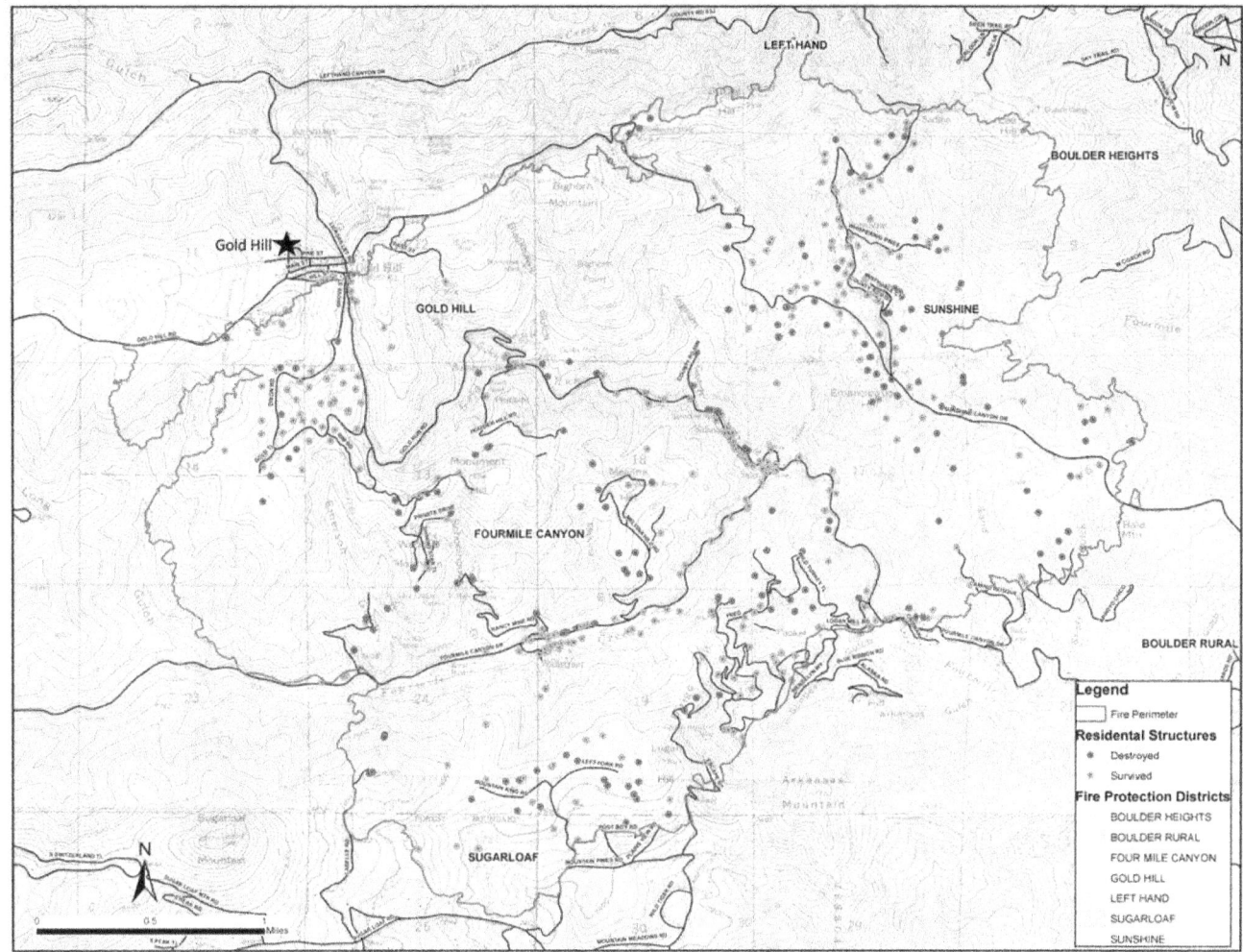

Figure 12. Multiple fire districts provide protection to the over 474 homes and other residential structures located within the area burned by the Fourmile Canyon Fire.

Pre-Fire

Boulder County is prepared for fire emergencies and has been building on the experience gained from past fire events in the county such as the Black Tiger Fire (1989), Olde Stage Fire (1990, 2009), Walker Ranch Fire (2001), and the Overland Fire (2003). In late 2009, Boulder County established a Type-3 Incident Management Team that was accepted by the State of Colorado in spring of 2010 as a fully operational team. The county also has an excellent infrastructure (e.g. building, phones, computers, etc.) to support major emergency events through the Boulder Emergency Operations Center. Reverse 911 capabilities for evacuation notification has existed since 2000. The local fire districts are prepared for emergencies and have conducted and rehearsed fire scenarios typical of the Fourmile Canyon Fire. The Fourmile Fire District exemplifies this preparedness by having physical maps for distribution to incoming units and to aid in evacuations.

Figure 13. A total of 474 homes were located in the area where the Fourmile Canyon Fire burned (photos: Russ Graham).

Antecedent Weather and Fire Danger

The weather prior to September 6 was normal to wetter-than-normal for most of the spring and summer of 2010 (Figure 14). Beginning in late August, a very dry and warm weather pattern emerged and September ended 4 °F above normal in temperature and about 1.5 inches below normal in precipitation. The Palmer Z-Index indicated that short-term moisture conditions in northern Colorado changed from moderately moist in July to severely dry by the end of September 2010. There are remote automated weather stations (RAWS) and several other weather stations located near the fire area (e.g., city of Boulder, Sugarloaf RAWS, Mesa Lab) that can be used to characterize the local weather during the Fourmile Canyon Fire (Figure 15). The last recorded precipitation prior to the fire at Sugarloaf RAWS was August 20, 17 days prior to the fire (Figure 16).

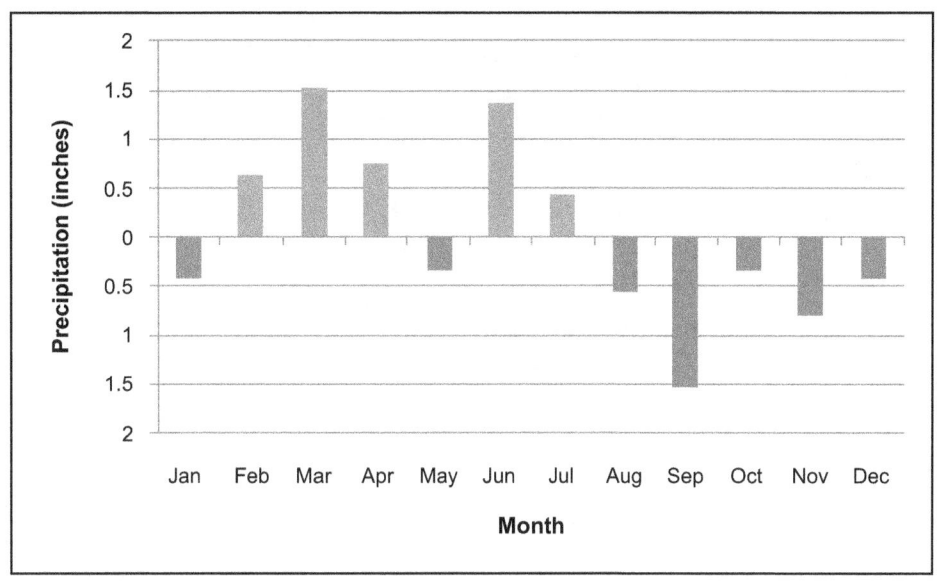

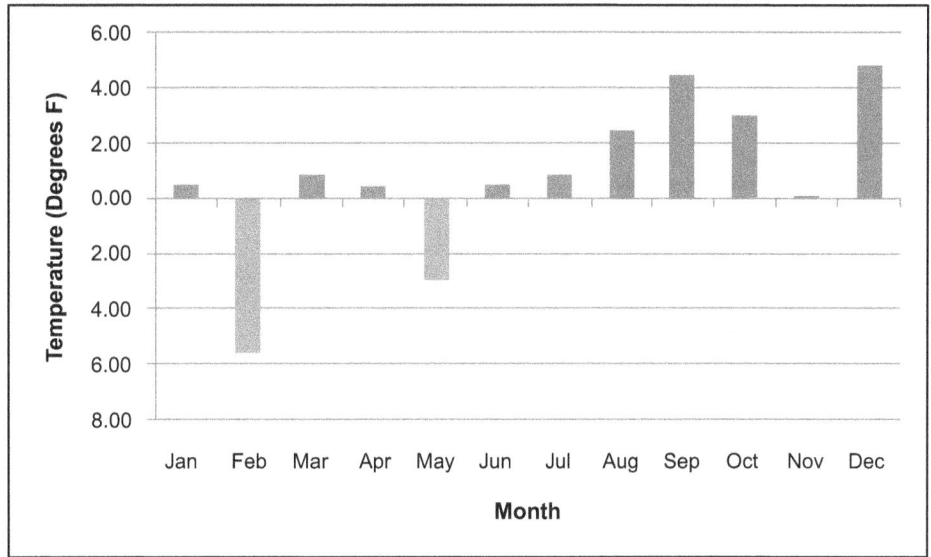

Figure 14. Based on the Boulder Co-op station (#050408), 2010 precipitation (inches) and temperature (degrees F) were mostly cool and wet February though July and then warm and dry from August through December compared to the 1971 through 2000 climate averages.

This weather pattern facilitated a rise in fire danger as expressed by the Energy Release Component (ERC) and Burning Index (BI) of the National Fire Danger Rating System (NFDRS) (Figure 17). ERC is typically a good seasonal dryness indicator that does not include the day to day variability of wind speed, while the BI does include wind as an input. The fire danger rose from seasonal normal values in mid-August to record levels in early September when the fire started. These factors resulted in moisture contents of the dead fuels in the area where the fire burned dropping to their lowest values of the season.

USDA Forest Service Gen. Tech. Rep. RMRS-GTR-289. 2012

17

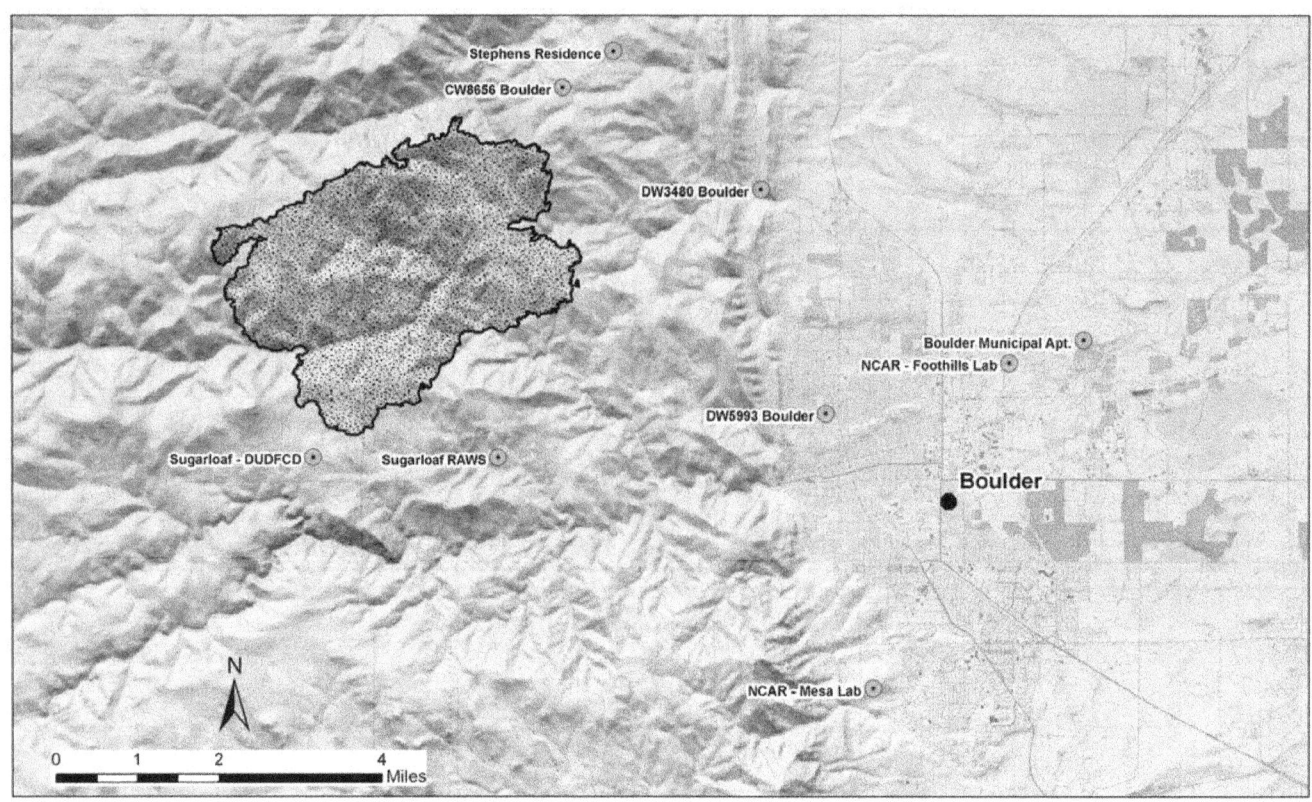

Figure 15. The location of remote automated weather stations (RAWS) and other weather stations located near the area where the Fourmile Canyon Fire burned.

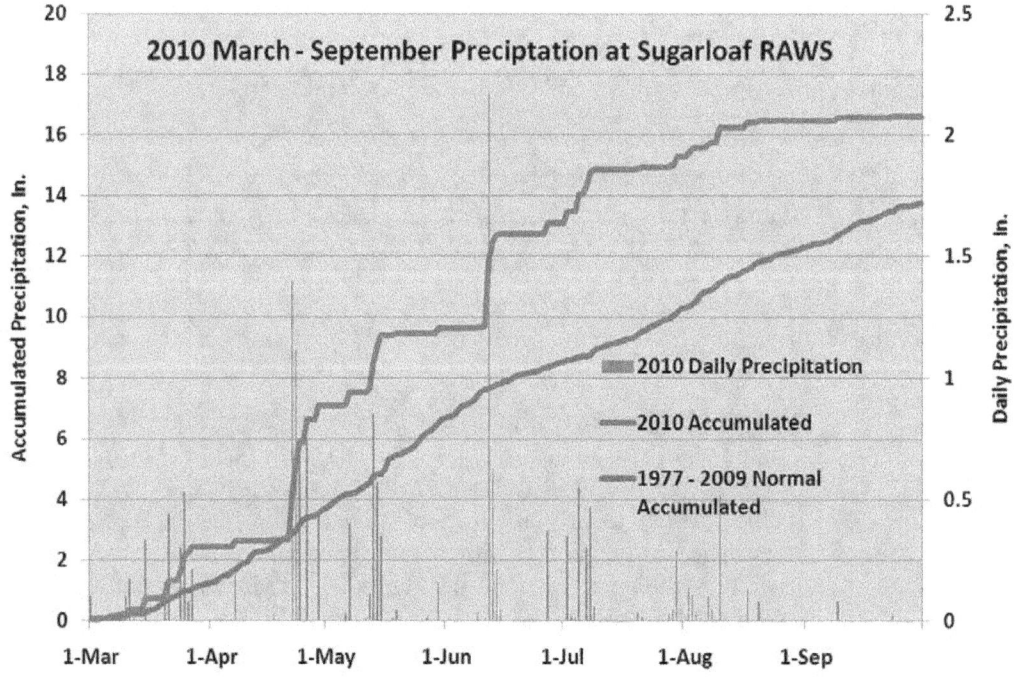

Figure 16. The daily and accumulated precipitation falling at the Sugarloaf remote automated weather Station (RAWS) along with the 1977 through 2009 average precipitation accumulation.

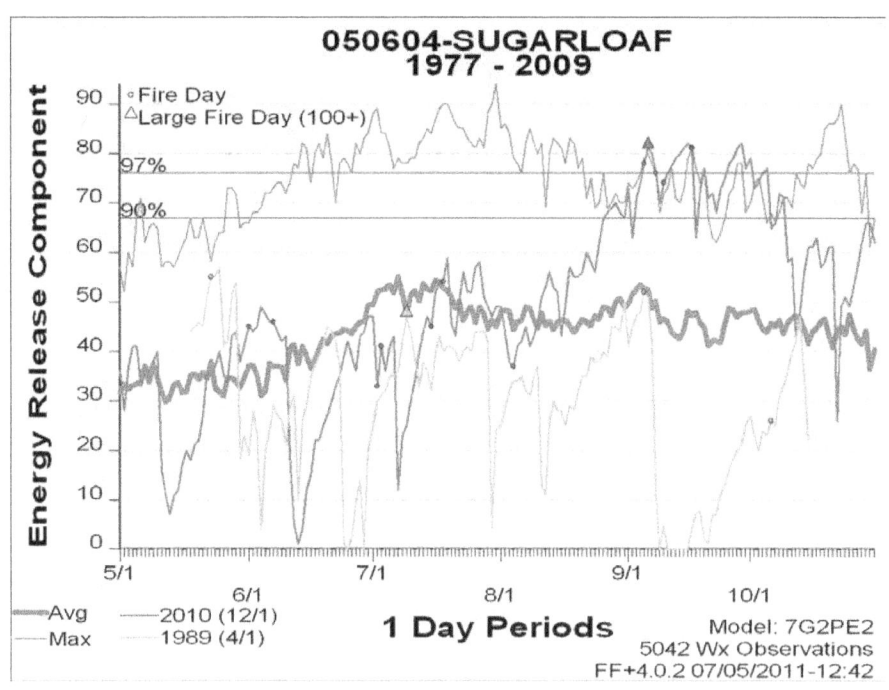

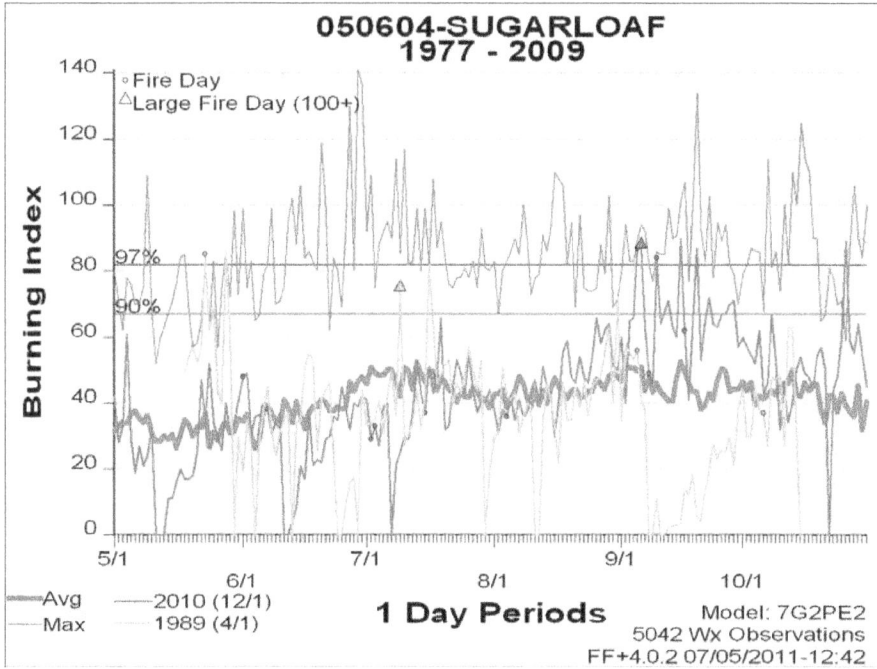

Figure 17. Fire danger as expressed by Energy Release Component (ERC) and Burning Index (BI) from Sugarloaf RAWS. The 2010 ERC trace (pink) shows steadily increasing fire danger in August. When the Fourmile Canyon Fire started it was just above the all-time high for that date and remained elevated through mid-October. The BI, which includes wind speed, shows less seasonal increase but a 2-day peak on September 5 and 6. The seasonal traces for 1989 (blue) contrasts conditions between the Black Tiger and Fourmile Canyon Fires.

USDA Forest Service Gen. Tech. Rep. RMRS-GTR-289. 2012

19

Winds

At 20 feet above ground level, the Sugarloaf RAWS measures both a 10-minute average wind speed and maximum (gust) wind speed occurring each hour. On September 6, the 10-minute average winds ranged from 6 to 15 miles per hour, while every hour between 0700 and 1600 a wind gust from the west exceeded 20 miles per hour. The maximum gust (41 mph) and maximum average (15 mph) wind speeds for the day both occurred the hour (1000 to 1100) the Fourmile Canyon Fire was reported. These values exceed the 99th percentile 10-minute average and maximum wind speeds of 13 and 29 miles per hour, respectively, that have been recorded at the Sugarloaf RAWS since it began collecting in June 2001 (Figure 15).

Winds can be highly altered by complex topography such as that in the area where the Fourmile Canyon Fire burned. WindWizard (Forthofer 2007), an adaptation of a Computational Fluid Dynamics (CFD) model, can show how topography affects local wind flow. Visualizations from WindWizard are not forecasts. Rather they are high resolution simulations of how fine-scale wind flow can vary with different prevailing wind speeds and direction in complex terrain. In this case, using 30 meter spatial resolution, even though the predominant winds were blowing from the west over the fire area (i.e., Sugarloaf RAWS), within the canyons and draws many wind directions and speeds were possible depending on location. Also, the higher winds (35 mph or greater) occurred at the ridge tops especially above Fourmile and Gold Creeks (Figures 4, 18). These multi directional and strong winds were especially evident near the mouth of Emerson Gulch where the fire started (Figure 19).

Figure 18. Wind directions displayed (modeled) using the WindWizard software for the Fourmile Canyon Fire area. Note the faster winds (red) blowing along ridges within the area.

Figure 19. Wind directions displayed (modeled) using the WindWizard software for the Fourmile Canyon Fire focusing on where the fire started near the mouth of Emerson Gulch. Note the faster winds (red) blowing along the ridges.

Fuel Treatments

The intent of fuel treatments is to change fuel structure and composition so when wildfires burn their behavior is manageable (e.g., fire can be suppressed, controlled, contained) or the burn severity (fire effects) is of a desirable nature (e.g., intact homes, green trees, resilient soils). The efficacy of fuel treatments to produce desired outcomes depends on how the live and dead vegetation are treated (e.g., vegetation cut, piled, burned, masticated), time since treatment, and how the treated areas are dispersed, shaped, and arranged across the landscape. Wildland fuel treatments have been documented and studied for 80-plus years (Weaver 1943, Pollet and Omi 2002, Graham and others 2004, Agee and Skinner 2005, Finney and others 2005, Cram and others 2006, Hunter and others 2007, Graham and others 2009, Hudak and others 2011). A large proportion of this evidence applies directly to the ponderosa pine and mixed conifer forests of the Colorado Front Range and the Fourmile Canyon area. This body of knowledge unequivocally demonstrates that changes in fire behavior and subsequent effects are most dependent on changes in surface fuels. In fact, very effective fuel treatment in many studies consists solely of prescribed burning with no overstory tree removal (e.g., Hayman Fire, Finney and others 2003). Canopy treatments start with removing ladder fuels (e.g., shrubs, small trees) and raising the crown base height of standing trees by pruning the lowest branches to limit transition from surface to crown fire (Figure 20).

USDA Forest Service Gen. Tech. Rep. RMRS-GTR-289. 2012

21

Figure 20. The most effective strategy for reducing crown fire occurrence and burn severity is to (1) reduce surface fuels D, E, F; (2) remove ladder fuels B, C; (3) increase canopy base heights A; (4) and lastly, reduce canopy continuity and density A (photos: Russ Graham).

Thinning overstory trees to increase spacing between tree crowns and decreasing continuity of aerial fuels can be used to decrease the potential for an independent crown fire. The state of knowledge clearly supports the generalization that canopy treatments alone produce minimal effects on fire behavior or reductions in burn severity to residual trees. It is recognized that thinning followed by removing the surface fuels, most often by prescribed broadcast burning, produces the most durable treatment benefits (Graham and others 1999, 2004).

Approximately 600 acres (9.7% of the burned area) of fuel treatments located within the final fire perimeter were conducted between 2004 and 2010. Four-hundred and seventeen acres (417) of these fuel treatments were administered by the Colorado State Forest Service. However 113 of these 417 acres were on Bureau of Land Management lands (Figure 21). Additionally, 21 acres of treatment were conducted by the U.S. Forest Service in the Sugar Loaf area and another 162 acres of treatments with unknown locations were distributed throughout the area. These treatments were also administered by the Colorado State Forest Service and consisted of mainly defensible space projects around individual homes. Boulder County Parks and Open Space (BCPOS) also conducted work in the area northeast of Gold Hill and in the area of Bald Mountain.

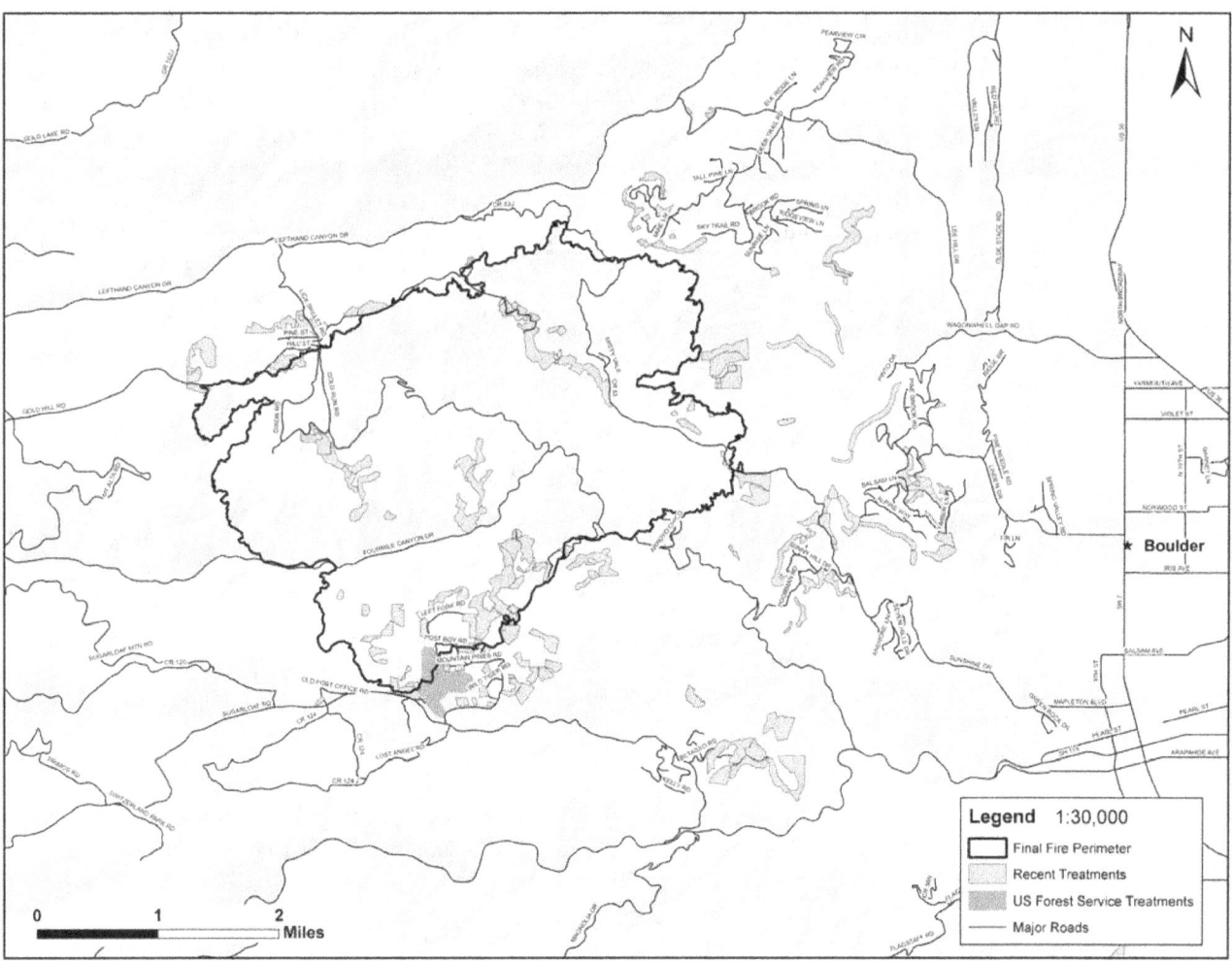

Figure 21. A total of 417 acres of fuel treatment had documented geospatial locations within the area where the Fourmile Canyon Fire burned. The treated areas were located near homes, along ridge-tops, and along roads. An additional 162 acres of treatments did not have geospatial locations and are not shown here. These treatments were mainly defensible space projects surrounding individual homes. Twenty one acres of U.S. Forest Service treatments were also within the fire perimeter.

USDA Forest Service Gen. Tech. Rep. RMRS-GTR-289. 2012

23

There are likely additional treatments that were performed by homeowners throughout the area, which we could not account for. We found no evidence that broadcast burning of surface fuels (e.g., grasses, twigs, limbs, needles) occurred in the area where the fire burned. Fuel treatment prescriptions obtained from Colorado State Forest Service showed the following treatments:

- Thinning from below by removing small trees;
- Chipping the small-diameter limbs on the forest floor;
- Piling and burning of limbs and the boles of small trees; and
- Piling but not burning the boles of the large trees removed in the thinnings.

The condition of fuels in treatment units at the time of the Fourmile Canyon Fire is not known but would depend on the original treatment prescription, fuel accumulation since the treatment occurred, and regrowth of vegetation. All of these would vary among treatment units. Pre- and post-treatment photographs were helpful in documenting the nature of some treatments, especially the thinning effects (e.g., tree removal) that were readily visible (Figure 22). Treatment units that had not burned during the Fourmile Canyon Fire, but were recorded as receiving treatments similar to those nearby areas that had burned, were inspected and suggested an abundance of continuous surface fuels were present in the treated areas. These fuels consisted of grass, litter, dead woody material, brush, small trees, and in some cases piles of large woody material (Figure 23). Canopy and understory thinning increased the spacing between overstory trees and made the forest more open (Figure 24). However, under the wildfire weather conditions experienced routinely in the Colorado foothills, high fire spread rates (0.5 to 1.0 mph) and high fire intensities (flame lengths of 5 to 10 feet) would be expected. Such intensities would be sufficient to ignite and entirely consume the leaves/needles of the residual overstory trees (Figure 25) (Scott and Burgan 2005).

Fuels were also treated along several roads in the area. In general, these treatments extended to 150 feet on both sides of the road providing a 300-foot wide roadside treatment (Figure 21). Where applicable and feasible, these roadside treatments were connected to treatments located near homes and were designed and implemented to offer the following benefits:

- Create road corridors that allow safe travel for homeowners leaving and fire-fighters entering a wildfire area;
- Create a wildfire defendable zone using a shaded fuel break consisting of moderate to low tree densities with no ladder fuels near homes and communities;
- Improve forest health by increasing tree vigor through removal of excess and unhealthy trees;
- Enhance existing quaking aspen (*Populus tremuloides*) clones by greatly reducing the number of conifers in and among the quaking aspen stands; and
- Improve wildlife habitat by creating debris piles and encouraging the development of native grasses.

Hand-falling of trees with chainsaws was the most common method of removing ladder fuels and decreasing tree canopy densities. Within 50 feet of roads, the small material (3 inches diameter and less) was often chipped creating a layer of chips 6 inches and less in depth. Outside of this area and within 75 feet of main roads or homes, the fine fuels were piled by hand. In some areas where slope steepness was less than 30 percent, the small trees were masticated (e.g., shredded, chunked, or munched by a machine) rather than hand-falling.

Figure 22. Examples of fuel treatments within the Fourmile Canyon Fire area. The top pictures show a forest thinned using a masticator (machine that chunks and shreds woody material). Bottom pictures show trees cut by hand and the fuels created by the treatment were chipped. The pre-existing surface fuels were not treated in either unit (photos: Bob Bundy).

USDA Forest Service Gen. Tech. Rep. RMRS-GTR-289. 2012

25

Figure 23. Abundant grasses, shrubs, fine woody, and occasionally small trees and wood piles dominated the surface fuels in areas where fuels had been treated, as illustrated by treated areas adjacent to the fire perimeter that did not burn (photos: Mark Finney).

26

USDA Forest Service Gen. Tech. Rep. RMRS-GTR-289. 2012

Figure 24. Both of these photos illustrate how tree thinning used in the fuel treatments appreciably increased the distance between tree crowns (photos: Chuck McHugh).

USDA Forest Service Gen. Tech. Rep. RMRS-GTR-289. 2012

27

This assessment did not find documentation that described the intended treatment performance, either in terms of changes to wildfire behavior under a targeted set of weather conditions, the intended use of treatments by fire suppression resources, or a possible strategic role of treatments in changing fire progression. Long-term maintenance of treatments for re-growth and understory response was not mentioned.

Figure 25. Widely spaced trees can readily ignite and burn when crowns extend down to the forest floor near surface fuels. Top photo shows the fire torching trees in the early afternoon on September 6 along Fourmile Canyon Drive and the bottom photo shows the fire burning near Sunshine Canyon Drive in the early evening on September 6 (photos: Molly Wineteer (top); Mike Tombolato (bottom)).

28

USDA Forest Service Gen. Tech. Rep. RMRS-GTR-289. 2012

Fourmile Canyon Fire

Fire Weather

On September 6, the weather conditions that directly affected the Fourmile Canyon Fire were controlled by the synoptic (large scale) atmospheric conditions. On Sunday, September 5, a low pressure system began moving south and east from western Canada into the Rocky Mountains of the United States (Figure 26A). This system brought a very dry air mass onto the Colorado Front Range and the fire area (Figure 26B).

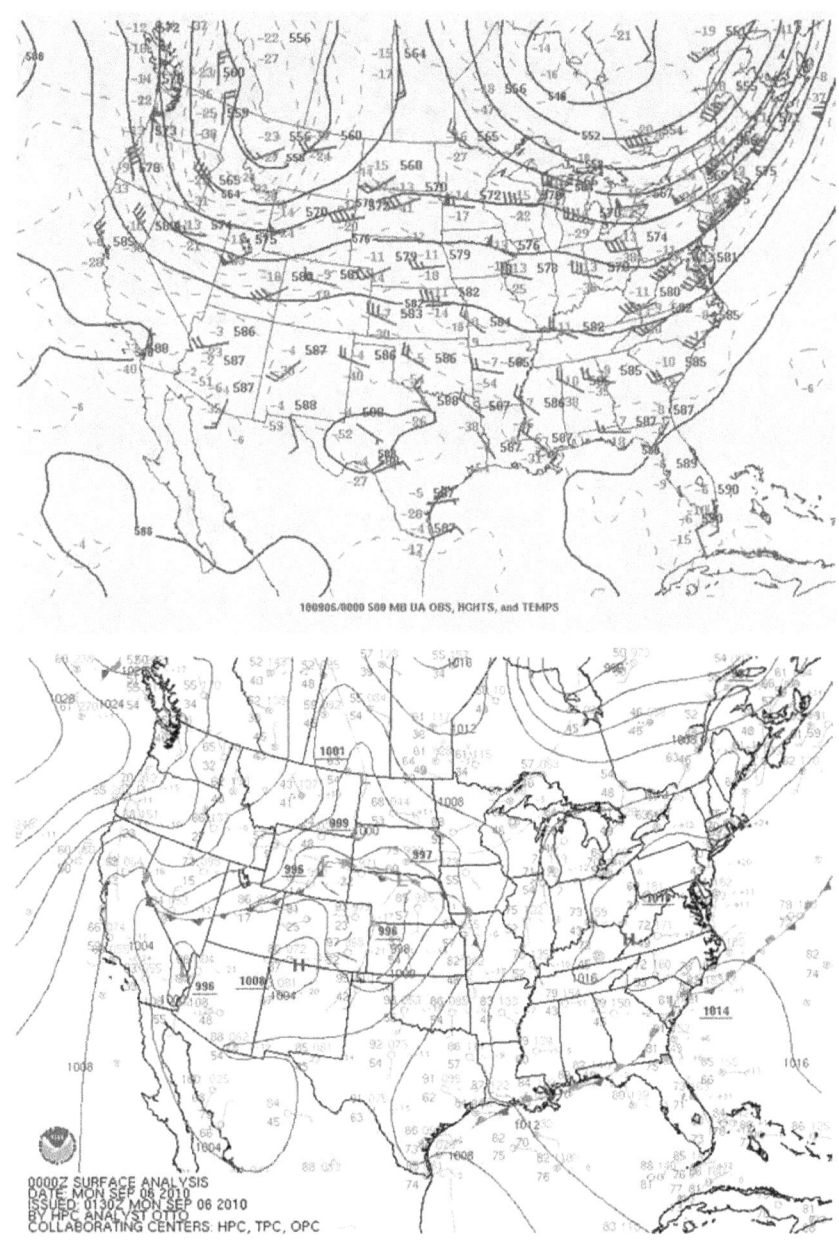

Figure 26 A and B. Synoptic (large scale) weather summary for the contiguous United States showing (A) upper air pressure and wind (500 mb) and (B) surface weather for September 5, 2010 at 1800 MDT.

USDA Forest Service Gen. Tech. Rep. RMRS-GTR-289. 2012

29

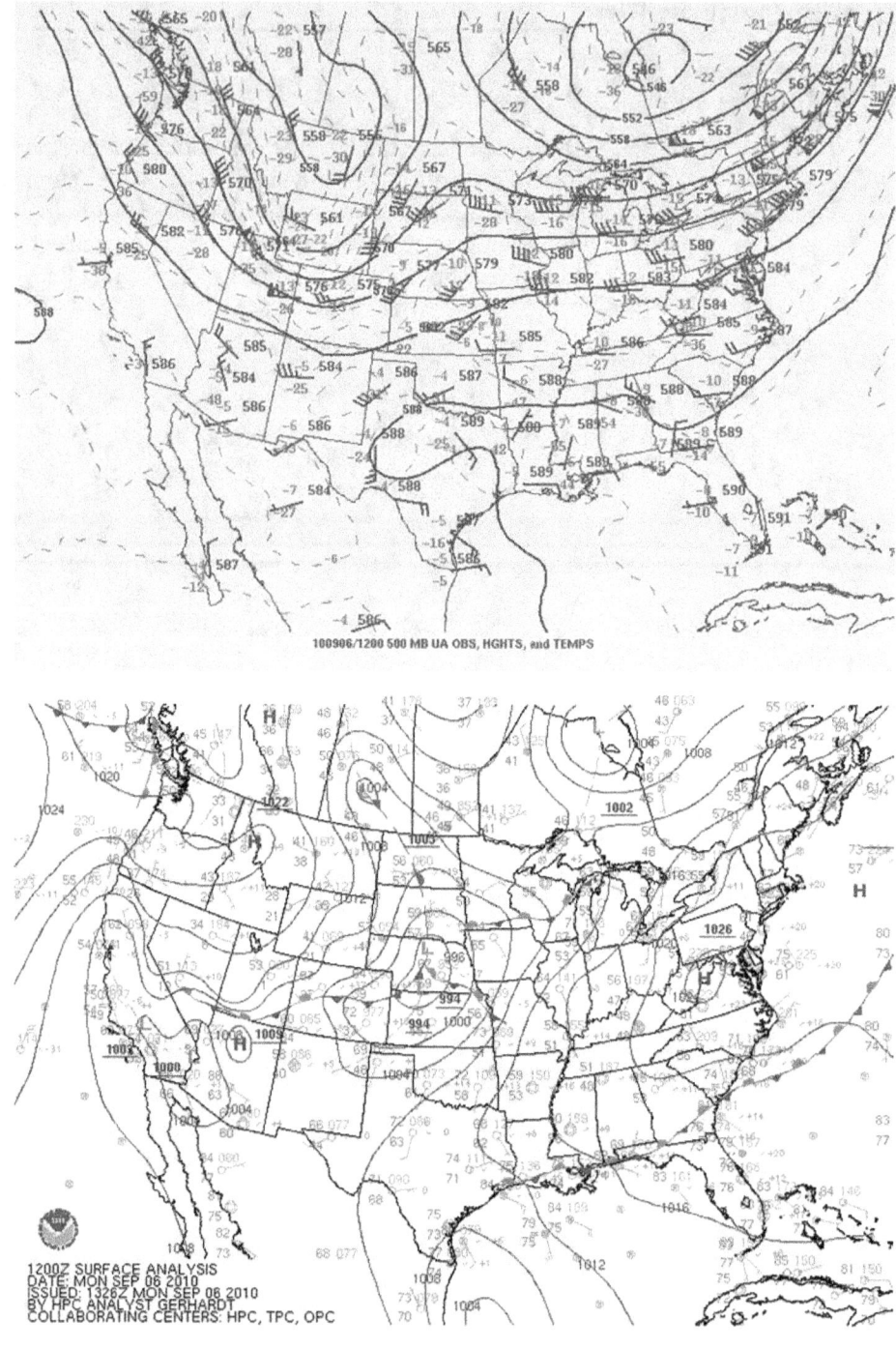

Figure 26 C and D. Synoptic (large scale) weather summary for the contiguous United States showing (C) upper air pressure and wind (500 mb) and (D) surface weather for September 6, 2010 at 0600 MDT.

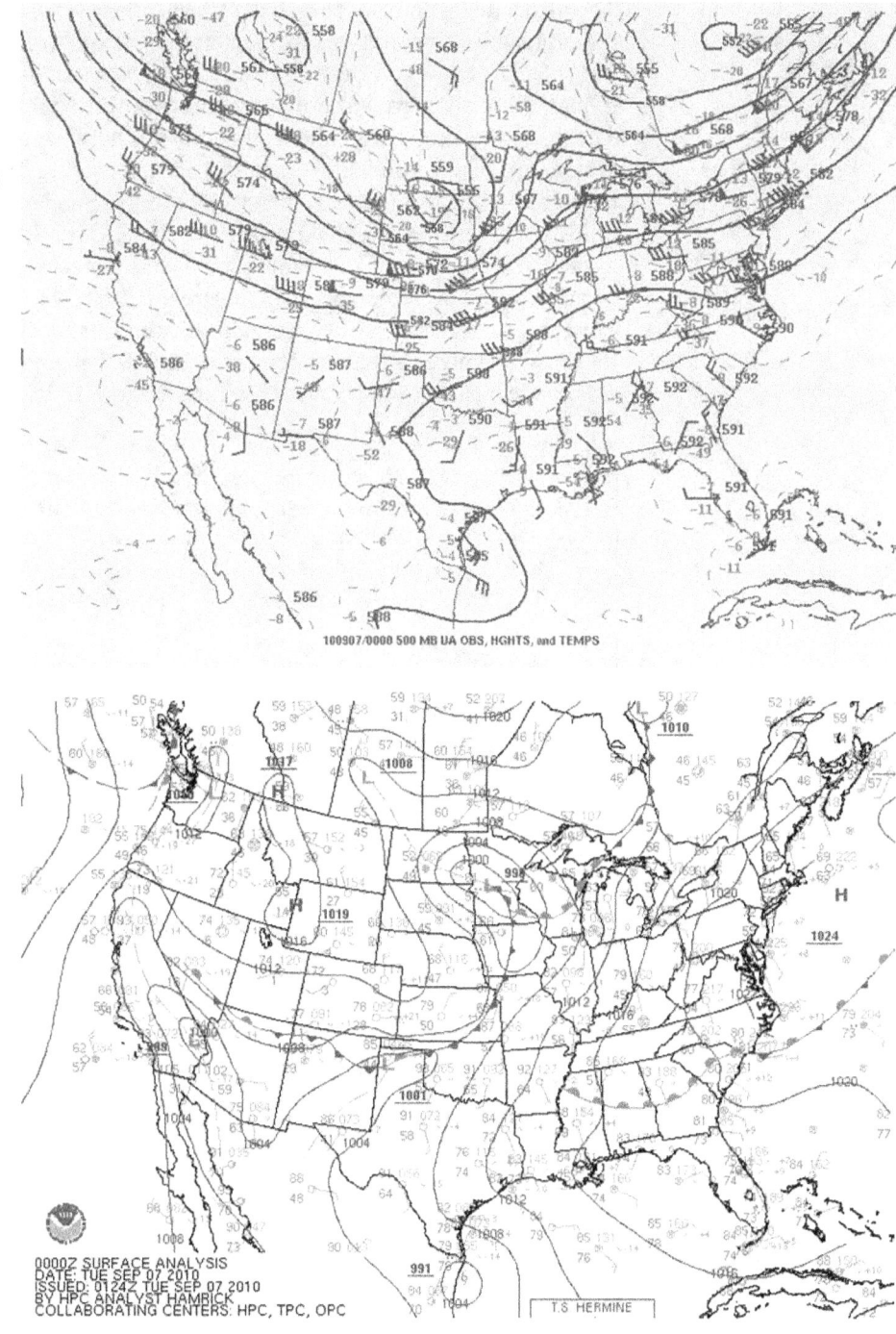

100907/0000 500 MB UA OBS, HGHTS, and TEMPS

0000Z SURFACE ANALYSIS
DATE: TUE SEP 07 2010
ISSUED: 0124Z TUE SEP 07 2010
BY HPC ANALYST HAMBRICK
COLLABORATING CENTERS: HPC, TPC, OPC

T.S. HERMINE

Figure 26 E and F. Synoptic (large scale) weather summary for the contiguous United States showing (E) upper air pressure and wind (500 mb) and (F) surface weather for September 6, 2010 at 1800 MDT.

USDA Forest Service Gen. Tech. Rep. RMRS-GTR-289. 2012

31

The associated cold front passed the fire area early Monday morning, around 0100 and brought cooler temperatures for September 6 compared to those on September 5 (Figure 26C, D). However, overnight air humidity at the Sugarloaf RAWS only recovered to the mid-thirties from afternoon values below 10 percent observed on September 5. The tightening pressure gradient along the southern edge of the advancing low-pressure system resulted in much higher wind speeds, changing from about 18 miles per hour at the upper-levels of the atmosphere (500 mb) on Sunday evening in Denver to over 60 miles per hour Monday evening (Figures 26 A, C, E, 27 A). This synoptic pattern also led to the development of a mountain wave with accelerating westerly surface winds during the day of September 6 (Kriederman 2010). Along with the high winds, the atmosphere was extremely dry. Soundings from Denver showed the relative humidity of the air was likely less than 10 percent at 12,000 feet above the fire on Monday evening, a dramatic change from Monday morning (Figure 27 B). Hourly traces of humidity and

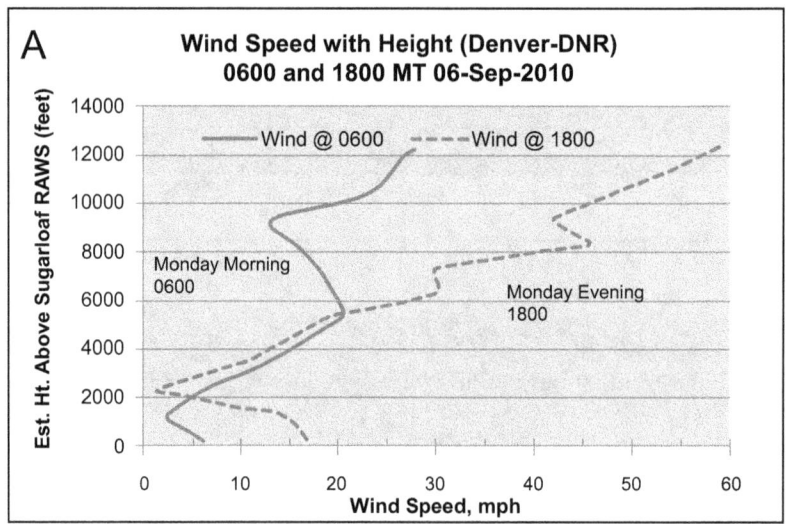

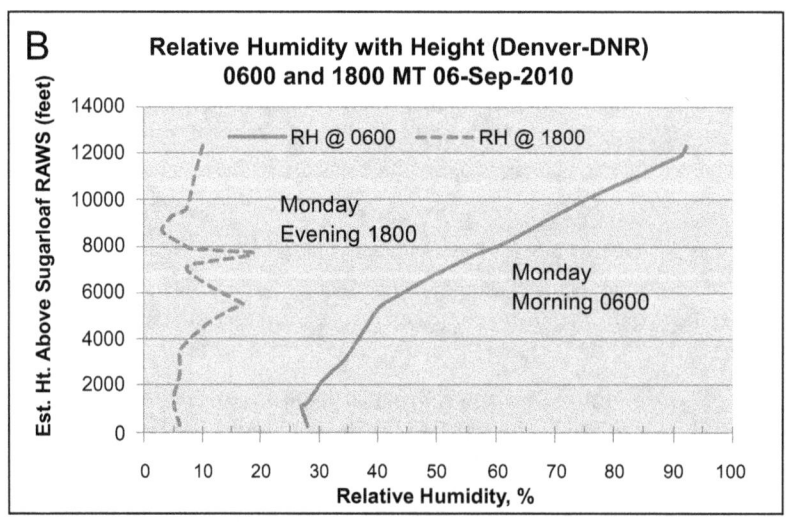

Figure 27. Morning and evening atmosphere soundings from Denver, Colorado, on Monday, September 6, 2010, showing (A) a dramatic drying of the entire atmosphere, and (B) a significant increase in winds at the surface and for winds 5,000 feet above the fire.

wind speed at the Sugarloaf RAWS show extreme fire weather conditions for both Sunday September 5 and Monday September 6 (Figure 28). At the time the fire was reported, the air relative humidity was 7 percent and the 10-minute average wind speed was 15 miles per hour and gusting to 41 miles per hour. The air relative humidity dropped to 4 percent from about 1400 to 1700 and the sustained winds remained strong with gusts ranging from 25 to 30 miles per hour. Between 1700 and 1800 winds turned easterly, abated in speed and gustiness, and the air humidity rose from 4 to 14 percent. Figure 28 also indicates steadily moderating fire weather conditions for Tuesday through Thursday when the air relative humidity did not drop below 15 percent and wind gusts did not exceed 20 miles per hour. Similar weather conditions prevailed at each of the other weather stations located near where the fire burned (Figure 15).

Initial Response

An emergency 911 call at 1002 on Monday September 6 reported a fire located near the mouth of Emerson Gulch, where the Gulch intersects with Fourmile Canyon (Figures 3, 29). With the multiple Fire Protection Districts in the area, numerous engines and personnel responded to the fire as well as units from Colorado State Forest Service, U.S. Forest Service, Boulder County, and the City of Boulder. The control of incoming resources into the fire area, life-safety (firefighter and public), and evacuations were a major concern of the initial attack Incident Commander and the subsequent Type-3 Incident Commander. The Type-3 Incident Management Team (IMT) was dealing with evacuations late (2100) into the evening on September 6 (personal communication, Don Whittemore, Incident Commander, Type-3 Boulder Incident Management Team).

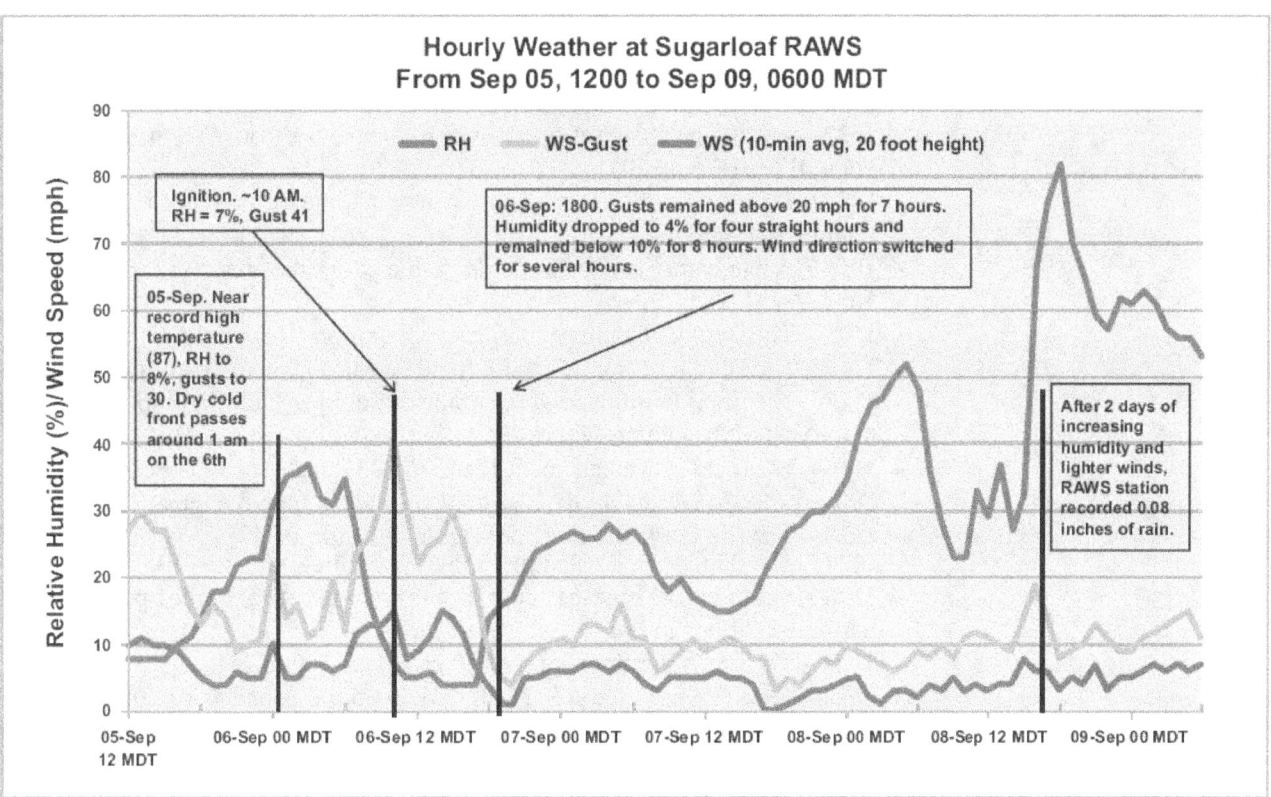

Figure 28. September 5 had air relative humidity (RH) below 10 percent from 1100 to 1800 and wind gusts between 20 and 30 miles per hour until 1600. A cold front passed the fire area around 0100 on September 6 creating gusty winds but RH only recovered to mid-30s. By 1000 on the September 6, RH dropped to 7 percent. A wind gust of 41 miles per hour was recorded the hour the Fourmile Canyon Fire was reported. Sustained winds blew ranging from 9 to 15 miles per hour until 1700.

The response of multiple resident resources also overwhelmed the local communication systems. Setting up staging areas and establishing command and control of resources coming into and within the area were critical for firefighter and public safety. Responding units found this delay frustrating (BIMT 2010). However, it likely contributed to the overall safety of firefighters and the general public during the first day of the fire. During the initial attack of the fire, a series of trigger points were established for the initiation of evacuations. However, the fire was moving so fast that these trigger points were often over-run before the actions could be fully initiated. Notifications of evacuations were conducted by Boulder County Sheriff Officer's, on-scene fire personnel, and through the utilization of reverse 911 calls. Because of this early focus on the control of incoming resources, evacuations, and life-safety, fire suppression mainly concentrated on protection of structures where feasible rather than fire containment.

The following is a summary for the first 13 hours of the radio dispatch and 911 call transcripts from the Boulder County Sheriff's Office and the WildCAD Incident Log from the Fort Collins Interagency Dispatch Center:

- 1002—The fire is reported on Monday September 6 and there is confusion as to the cause of the fire (Figure 29).
- 1013—An inquiry is made about the availability of air tankers.
- 1015—A single engine air tanker (SEAT) is located at Fort Collins, Colorado; one large air tanker is located in Grand Junction, Colorado, and another in Rapid City, South Dakota.
- 1021—Fort Collins dispatch advises that wind conditions will not allow the use of air tankers at this time.
- 1023—Fourmile Fire District units arrive on the scene, establish command, and start sizing up the fire.
- 1026—The fire had already spotted to the west across the Emerson Gulch Road from where it started (Figure 29).
- 1037—A staging area is set-up for incoming resources on Wall Street west of the old mill site (Figure 29).
- 1041—Flames from below are approaching a home located on a ridge top at 300 Shining Star Trail.
- 1055—A mandatory evacuation order is issued for the area.
- 1056—A SEAT is ordered.
- 1108—The Boulder County Emergency Operations Center (EOC) is opened.
- 1114—The Boulder County Type-3 Incident Management Team is ordered.
- 1115—The fire is burning on the east side of Emerson Gulch and spotting 0.5 mile to the east of the Gulch (Figure 29).
- 1116—The Incident Management Team (IMT-3) located at 5901 Fourmile Canyon Drive, orders six structure defense engines and six type-6 engines (Figure 29).
- 1123—The fire crests the ridge near Gold Hill (Figure 29).
- 1124—The flames are located just above Wall Street (Figure 29).
- 1128—Sustained 10 mile per hour winds and gusts to 20 miles per hour create unsafe conditions to fly.
- 1129—The fire is burning along Melvina Road (Figure 29).
- 1132—The fire is reported at 531 Left Fork Road and a home is burning (Figure 29).
- 1133—Incident Command Post (ICP) and staging area are moved to the Boulder Mountain Lodge.
- 1133—The power is shut off in Fourmile Canyon.

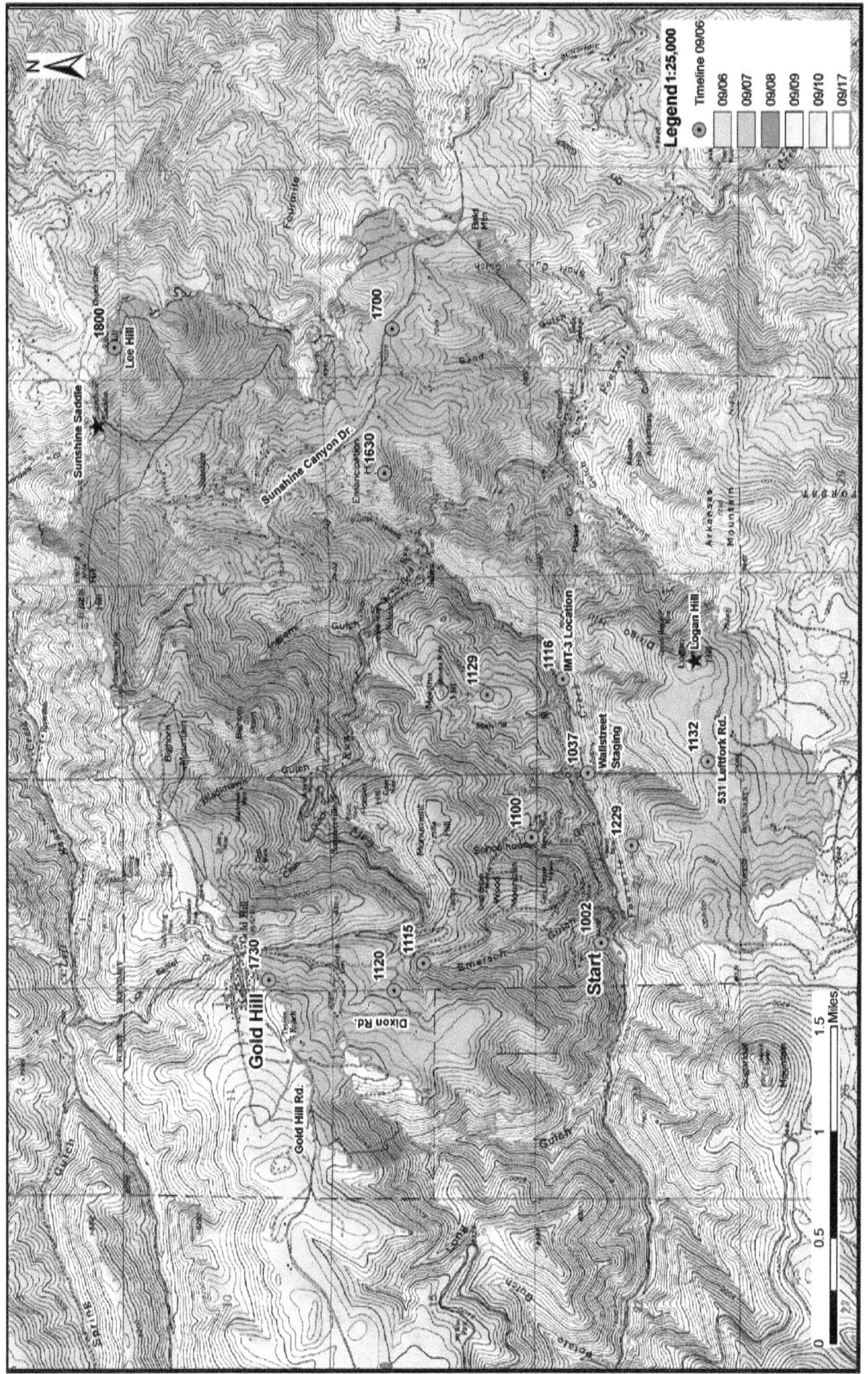

Figure 29. Daily progression of the Fourmile Canyon Fire. The points show the documented fire arrival times on September 6.

- 1142—Three houses confirmed destroyed on Melvina Hill Road (Figure 29).
- 1158—A SEAT is unable to drop due to high winds.
- 1203—Incoming units respond to the Boulder County Justice Center (BCJC).
- 1208—Reverse 911 calls initiated for the Mountain Meadows area between Arkansas Mountain Road and Sugarloaf and Left Fork roads (Figure 29).
- 1211—A SEAT jettisons its load and lands at Jeffco Air Tanker Base.
- 1213—The fire is burning near a house at 6556 Fourmile Canyon Road.
- 1213—The Incident Command Post and staging area are moved to the Boulder County Justice Center.
- 1216—Reverse 911 calls are issued for a 3-mile radius around Gold Hill (Figure 29).
- 1217—An order is placed for three Type-1 crews.
- 1229—The fire is continuing to move rapidly. It has crossed Wall Street and climbing up the south side of the slope (Figure 29).
- 1230—The Boulder Incident Management Team is ordered.
- 1237—Control of the fire along Mountain King Road is lost.
- 1241—The fire is burning along Logan Mill Road.
- 1315—The fire has crossed Gold Hill Road (Figure 29).
- 1300—A Type-3 Incident Management Team (IMT-3) assumes responsibility for the fire.
- 1306—Large air tankers are ordered from Grand Junction, Colorado, and Rapid City, South Dakota.
- 1308—The Colorado Mountain Ranch is evacuated.
- 1349—Large air tanker T-25 is leaving Grand Junction, Colorado.
- 1356—Rocky Mountain Incident Management Team, A Richardson's Type-2 IMT is ordered.
- 1402—Large air tanker T-45 is leaving Rapid City, South Dakota.
- 1712—Air tanker operations start. Air tanker AT-878 is in route to the fire from Jefferson County (Jeffco) Air Tanker Base, Broomfield, Colorado.
- 1722—Air tanker T-25 is in route to the fire from Jeffco Air Tanker Base.
- 1731—Air tanker T-45 is in route to the fire from Jeffco Air Tanker Base.
- 1953—Air tanker operations cease. Air tankers T-25, T-45, and AT-878 all returning to Jeffco Air Tanker Base.
- 2256—Thomas's Type-1 IMT is ordered.

Fire Behavior

The Fourmile Canyon Fire was reported at approximately 1002 on Monday September 6 near the mouth of Emerson Gulch (Figure 29). Fire investigators determined it was started by an escape from a burning pile of debris located on private property. The burning pile occurred on the east side of the Emerson Gulch Road and a few hundred yards north of where it intersects with Fourmile Canyon Drive (Figure 29). Initial responders (including, but not limited to, Boulder County Sherriff's Office, Fourmile Fire District, Sugarloaf Fire District, Gold Hill Fire District, Sunshine Fire District, Colorado State Forest Service) reported flames spreading north and uphill on both sides of Emerson Gulch. When the fire started, winds were westerly at 15 miles per hour and gusting to 41 miles per hour and air relative humidity was 7 percent and decreasing (Figure 28). West winds and steep south facing slopes within Emerson Gulch encouraged the fire to spread mostly to the north and east (Figure 29). Hourly moisture concentration of 1-hour fine fuels was estimated with Nelson's dead fuel moisture model using weather readings from the Sugarloaf RAWS (Figure 15) (Nelson, 2000, Carlson and others 2007).

The 1-hour fuel moisture concentration at ignition was estimated at 5 percent and dropping to less than 2 percent around 1700. BehavePlus (Andrews and others 2008) was used to estimate probability of surface fuels being ignited by firebrands (e.g., wind carried burning materials) through the day and it ranged from 55 percent at 1000 to 90 percent at 1700. Observers noted rapid fire spread through the surface fuels in the open ponderosa pine forest with many trees torching (e.g., tree crowns fully engulfed in flames) and spot fires starting in advance of the fire front (Figure 30). Minimal tree damage or mortality caused by bark beetles was evident in the area where the fire burned. As such, bark beetle activity had little to no effect on the fuels within the area burned by the Fourmile Canyon Fire, the fire's behavior, or the final fire size.

Figure 30. The fire was spreading rapidly and burning with high intensity shortly after it started near the mouth of Emerson Gulch (photos: Molly Wineteer (top); Rod Moraga (bottom)).

36

USDA Forest Service Gen. Tech. Rep. RMRS-GTR-289. 2012

September 6, 1120—Within the first 90 minutes, the fire was approaching Rim Road, about 0.5 miles south of the town of Gold Hill (Figure 29). It was also estimated to have moved east of the Nancy Mine Road or perhaps halfway from the Nancy Mine Road to Melvina Road. The south-facing slopes were dominated by open ponderosa pine forests, with some tree patches containing closed canopies. Rocky Mountain juniper trees and common juniper shrubs were also present. Surface fuels in these ponderosa pine forests consisted of perennial grasses, cheat grass, mountain mahogany shrubs, and an abundant amount of pine needles and small branches (Figures 5-7). With these abundant surface fuels and their dry condition, the fire spread rapidly with frequent torching of overstory trees (Figures 25, 30). Continuous flame zones developed in the deep needle litter resulting in burning the crowns of many overstory trees (Figure 31). Active crown fire (e.g., fire moving from tree crown to tree crown) also occurred, primarily where the forests were of such density that continuous crown fire could be sustained (Figure 32). Within this same time-frame the fire spotted to the south side of Four Mile Creek from where it started and burned uphill torching and crowning the predominantly Douglas-fir tree canopies (Figure 29).

Figure 31. Deep flame zones developed beneath the ponderosa pine trees because of the continuous litter and woody surface fuels that burn for a much longer period of time than do grasses. This burning ultimately resulted in the igniting and torching of trees (photos: Mike Tombolato (top); Molly Wineteer (bottom)).

USDA Forest Service Gen. Tech. Rep. RMRS-GTR-289. 2012

37

Figure 32. Crown fires, fueled by abundant surface fuels, burned where dense and continuous tree crowns occurred (photos: Greg Cortopassi (top); Mike Tombolato (bottom)).

September 6, 1200—By noon on September 6, the fire burned to within a few hundred yards of Dixon Road on the north, crossed Melvina Road to the ridge west of Salina on the east, and was probably nearing the ridge west of Logan Hill to the south (Figure 29). It was estimated to be about 3,000 acres by the Incident Management Team. By 1200, despite the rapid progress to the east, the fire had not burned into the bottom of Fourmile Canyon. However, sometime after 1330 the fire was slowly backing down the south facing slope into Wall Street (Figures 29, 33). When the fire reached the ridge tops on the south and north sides of Fourmile Canyon, the fire front was fully exposed

Figure 33. Early afternoon on September 6, the fire was burning east of Emerson Gulch in the area of Wall Street. Top photo is at 7210 Fourmile Canyon Drive. Note these surface fires are backing down hill (photos: Molly Wineteer (top); Mike Tombolato (bottom)).

USDA Forest Service Gen. Tech. Rep. RMRS-GTR-289. 2012

39

to strong winds but lacked alignment with the canyon slopes and valley-channeled winds that resulted in such rapid spread rates earlier in the day. Spotting was prevalent from embers (e.g., burning needles, twigs) generated by the torching of trees and was estimated to be 0.5 miles ahead of the fire front (Figure 25). This spotting allowed the fire to overwhelm and breach the broken topography and fuel changes as the fire spread towards the east (Figure 29). In particular, along the ridge on the south side of Fourmile Canyon, abundant crown fire and torching occurred (Figures 5, 18, 29, 34).

Figure 34. Canyon and valley bottoms, for the most part, did not burn with high intensities. The top scene is an example of high intensity burning on the slopes and ridges above the valley bottom in the Salina area along Gold Run Road. Homes above the bottoms had a greater chance for high intensity wildfire exposures (photo: Boulder County Sherriff Office). The bottom scene shows north-facing slopes that did not experience high intensity burning (photo: Chuck McHugh).

The north-facing slopes of Blackhawk Gulch, Cash Gulch, Gold Run, and smaller unnamed drainages north of Melvina Road exhibited much lower fire intensity than evident on the south facing slopes (Figure 29). Receiving less solar radiation and being dominated by short-needled Douglas-fir, these forests tend to contain more moisture than the ponderosa pine dominated forests in the area. In addition to being relatively moist, the topographic orientation of these forests was counter to the direction of the prevailing winds. Both conditions contributed to the low fire intensities observed (Figures 18, 19). This vegetation-topographic pattern was evident throughout the Fourmile Canyon Fire area and had more of an impact on how the fire burned than any effects the fuel modifications or suppression activities may have had. In fact, most of the north facing forests occurring along Fourmile Creek remained untouched by fire (Figure 34).

September 6, 1200-2000—The fire reached Sunshine Canyon Drive by 1400 spreading both as a surface fire and by spotting (Figure 29). At 1132 the fire had not reached Dixon Road and it took until 1730 to reach Gold Hill (Figure 29). The long-time required for the fire to move from Dixon Road to Gold Hill was probably because strong west winds kept the north edge of the fire a flanking fire (Figures 18, 29). Nevertheless, many trees torched as they had crowns low to the forest floor and there was abundant surface fuel (Figure 25). These fuel conditions produced long-duration and intense burning by the fire. At about 1630, the fire was burning actively on the south side of Sunshine Canyon Drive near Emancipation Hill (Figure 29). Most likely, by spotting to the north of Emancipation Hill, the fire crossed Sunshine Canyon Drive prior to 1630. Spotting advanced the fire to the communication antennas on Lee Hill by 1837 (at the extreme northeast corner of the fire) and burned most of the grassy slopes near the antennas (Figures 29, 35). This burning exemplifies how far the fire was able to spot as Lee Hill was disconnected from the main fire front, which was stalled near the bottom of Sunshine Canyon (Figure 29).

Figure 35. Burned grass surrounding the Lee Hill antennas after 1837 on September 6 (photo: Mike Tombolato).

Here again, because of topographic sheltering, the presence of Douglas-fir forests, and moderating weather conditions (increasing relative humidity and reduced wind speeds) the north facing slopes along Sunshine Canyon experienced low fire intensity and low burn severity. At the end of September 6 (or one burning period) the fire had burned approximately 5,733 acres or 93 percent of the total area burned by the fire.

September 7—The fire spread very little on September 7. The active fire that did occur was primarily burning islands of unburned vegetation left behind by the spot-driven fire spread of September 6. Some burning occurred on the fire perimeter near Buetzel Hill, the Lee Hill antenna site, and below Sunshine Saddle (Figure 29). This burning was primarily facilitated by the abundant fuels and the receptive topography that occurred in the area. Only 375 additional acres burned on September 7, increasing the fire size to 6,108 acres.

September 8—On September 8, the air relative humidity was higher and the air temperature cooler than on previous days and 0.08 inches of rain fell at the Sugarloaf RAWS near the end of the day (Figure 15). These conditions allowed additional fire control lines to be constructed and others strengthened. As a result, there was minimal fire growth and the fire size remained at 6,108 acres (Figure 29).

September 9—A Red Flag warning was issued for September 9 for high and gusty winds, high air temperatures, and low air relative humidity beginning at 1800. By 1500, the speed of westerly winds increased and the air relative humidity dropped below 20 percent (Figure 28). This caused the burning of surface fuels and the torching of trees that had not burned within the interior of the fire. South of Lee Hill and in the West Coach Road area, sustained winds of 40 miles per hour and a peak wind gust of 64 miles per hour were reported. These conditions created a spot fire about 2 to 3 acres in size outside of the control lines. This spot was the last fire expansion and the fire size at the end of the day was 6,131 acres, based on corrected infrared mapping (Figure 29).

September 10—The Red Flag warning that began on September 9 remained in effect for September 10 until 1800. Observed air relative humidity was in the mid-teens, air temperatures in the mid-60s to low 70s (degrees F), and peak wind gusts were blowing in the mid to high 20s (mph) during the afternoon. However, no significant fire growth occurred and the final fire size on September 10 was 6,181 acres based on corrected infrared mapping (Figure 29).

September 11 and Later—The fire did not increase in size after September 10 in spite of very unstable and dry air occurring over the fire area on September 12 and 13 as indicated by a forecasted Haines index of 6. In addition, strong west winds blew on September 15, which had minimal impact on fire growth. The fire was declared 100 percent contained on September 13.

Fire Suppression

Multiple data sources were employed to describe the suppression activities used on the Fourmile Canyon Fire. For aerial resources, geospatial drop locations were obtained from the Operational Loads Monitoring (OLM) program (Figure 36). All U.S. Forest Service contracted large air tankers (LATs) collect these data. However, due to technical difficulties, these data were unavailable for Tanker-48 used on the Fourmile Canyon Fire. Single Engine Aerial Tankers (SEATS) were not included in the OLM program. Data from the Aviation Business System (ABS), the I-Suite incident data for the Fourmile Canyon Fire, daily use summaries submitted to the Fourmile Canyon Fire Incident Management Teams, and the daily load sheets from the air tanker bases

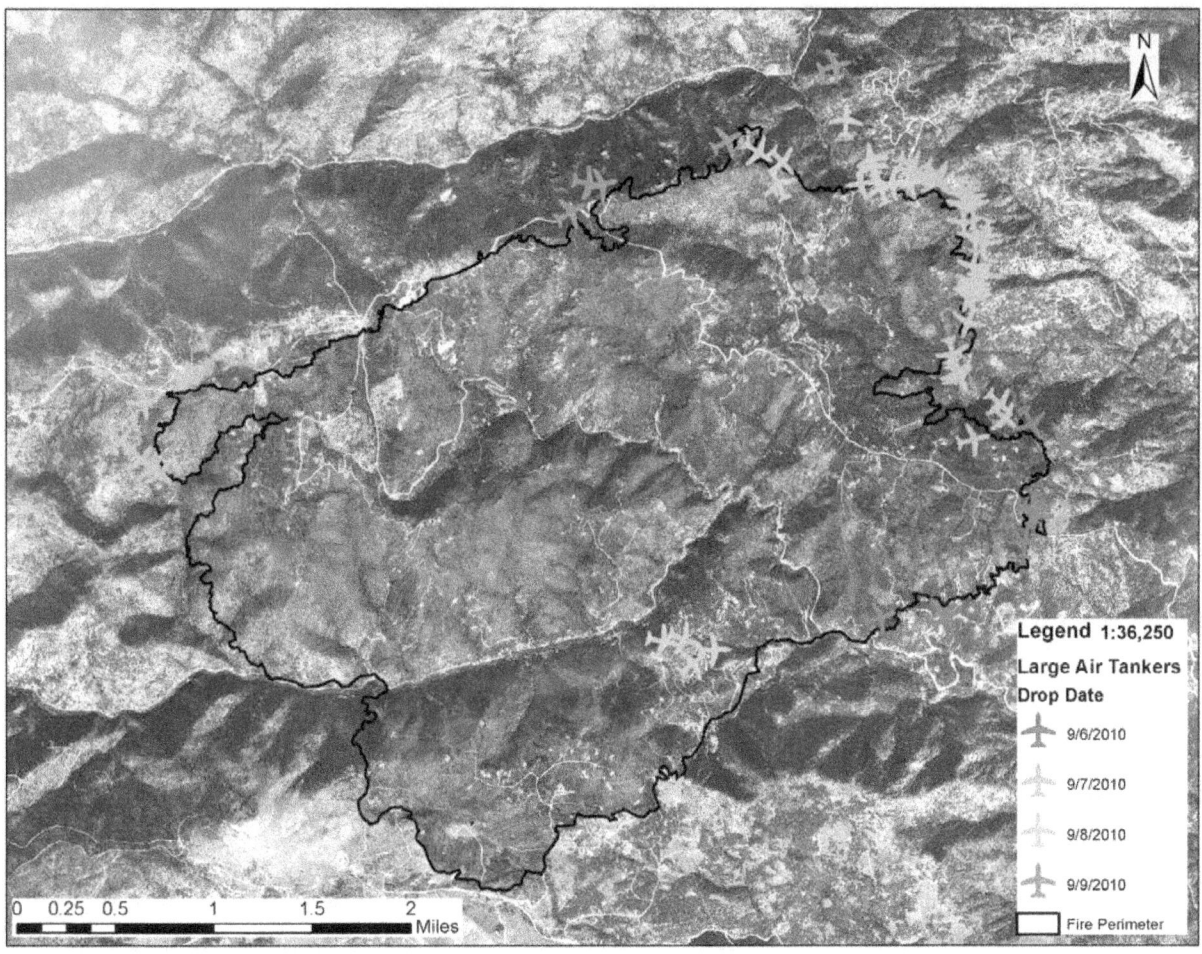

Figure 36. Summary of daily large air tanker activity on the Fourmile Canyon Fire. Black line is the final fire perimeter on September 17, 2010. The figure does not include helicopters, single engine air tankers (SEATS) or Tanker-48. Background is a WorldView satellite image from Digital Globe and is from September 12, 2010, at 1159.

were also incorporated. Additional information on suppression activities were obtained from the daily Incident Action Plans, Unit Logs, interviews with on-scene personnel, the Boulder County Type-3 Incident Management Team After Action Review, along with the incident narratives of Richardson's Type-2 Rocky Mountain Team A Incident Management Team, and Thomas's Type-1 Great Basin Incident Management Team.

September 6

When the fire was discovered on September 6, aircraft were ordered for initial attack. However, flying was unsafe due to wind speeds exceeding safe flying conditions and effective retardant use and all aircraft were grounded until 1700 (RMCG 2009, USDA-DOI 2011). A SEAT (AT-878) was ordered at 1056 but had to jettison its load and land at Jeffco Air Tanker Base because of the unsafe flying conditions. The fire was rapidly spreading in multiple directions (north towards Gold Hill, to the south towards Sugarloaf and to the east down Fourmile Canyon above Wall Street) and a consolidated suppression effort focusing on perimeter control could not be established (Figures 29-33). At this time, suppression efforts concentrated on evacuations, protection of structures when and where feasible, and the control and assignment of incoming resources (Figure 37).

By mid-afternoon isolated protection of homes by engines and crews was accomplished along Dixon Road, in the area of the Colorado Mountain Ranch, the town of Gold Hill, Sugarloaf area, and along the north side of Wall Street (Figures 9, 29, 37). It is quite likely that other isolated and undocumented point protection and suppression efforts occurred.

In the evening (1700) of September 6, the wind conditions moderated allowing aircraft to fly for approximately 3 hours. At 1730, tanker T-25 and AT-878, a SEAT, dropped retardant to the west of Gold Hill (Figure 38). These drops, in conjunction with

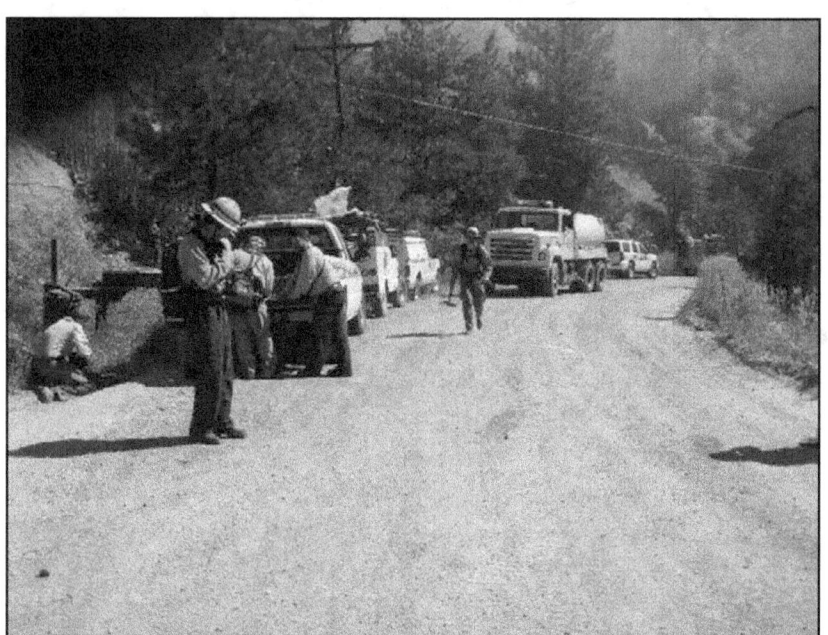

Figure 37. Managing and coordinating resources dispatched to the fire were major tasks during initial attack. Top scene shows the Emerson Gulch Incident Command Post and initial staging area on September 6, 2010 (photo: Mike Marzano). Bottom scene shows structure protection northeast of the Assay Office, Wall Street area on the afternoon of September 6, 2010 (photo: Molly Wineteer).

a wind shift (from west to east) and available ground resources, are attributed to saving Gold Hill from burning. Also, during the evening a total of nine loads were dropped by tankers T-25 and T-45 near Bald Mountain, located on the eastern perimeter of the fire (Figure 39). The retardant lines created by the air tankers connected to an area where the fuels had been treated in Boulder County Parks and Open Space lands. Drops were also made in the Camino Bosque and Arroyo Chico area (Figure 39). AT-878 also made five drops in the same areas between 1800 and 2000. A total of 25,605 gallons of retardant were dropped during this short period.

Figure 38. Top photo shows tanker T-25 making a drop adjacent to the town of Gold Hill at 1728 on September 6, 2010 (photo: Kurtis Leverentz). The bottom image shows the flight path of T-25 on the evening of September 6 adjacent to Gold Hill. The black arrow shows the general flight path of the drop. The purple color shows the retardant along the flight path. Background is a WorldView satellite image from Digital Globe taken on September 12, 2010 at 1159.

USDA Forest Service Gen. Tech. Rep. RMRS-GTR-289. 2012

45

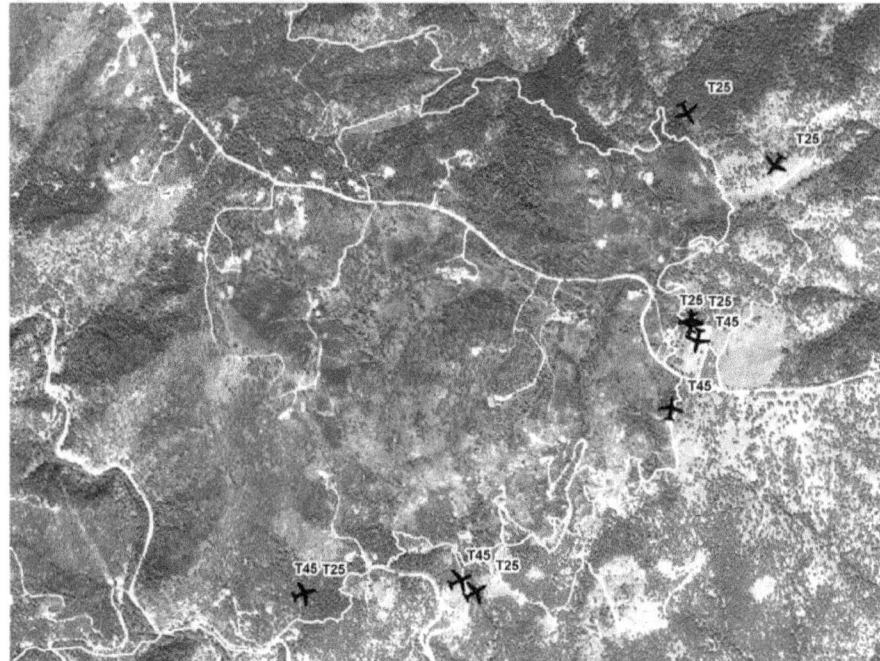

Figure 39. Top photo shows tanker T-25 heading towards the Bald Mountain Open space area on September 6, 2010 at 1800 hours (photo: Mark Leffingwell, Denver Post). Bottom image shows drops made in the Bald Mountain and Camino Bosque/Arroyo Chico area on September 6, 2010. Red areas along the fire edge are fire retardant. The white line shows the final fire perimeter on September 17, 2010. Background is a WorldView satellite image from Digital Globe taken September 12, 2010 at 1159.

September 7

On September 7, suppression concentrated on structure protection and occurred where fire behavior allowed for fire fighter safety. In particular, efforts were made to contain the fire south of Lefthand Canyon, east of Mount Alto, north of Boulder Creek, and west of Poorman, Sunshine, Pine Brook Hills, and Lee Hill (Figure 29). Ground crews worked to contain the fire in the area near Lee Hill and south towards Bald Mountain. Between 1300 and 1700 crews working along County Road 83 in the Whispering Pines and Sunshine area had to alternately disengage and reengage their structure protection several times. During this period, fire behavior was very erratic as the fire burned towards Butzel and to southeast of the Lee Hill antenna site. Also during this time, a strike team of engines working in the Church Camp area were ordered to withdraw to the Boulder Heights Fire District Station Number 2 because of the intense fire behavior (Figure 29). Air tankers were used heavily on the eastern flank during this time (Figure 37).

The flying conditions on September 7 were more favorable compared to those occurring on September 6 as a total of 44 loads (92,446 gallons or 53 percent the total) of retardant were dropped by one SEAT and seven air tankers. Between the hours of 1239 and 1617 numerous drops were made from Lee Hill south towards Bald Mountain on the eastern perimeter of the fire (Figures 37, 40). These eastern perimeter drops were

Figure 40. Retardant was dropped in the Lee Hill and Church Camp areas on the eastern perimeter of the fire on September 7 between 1239 and 1617. The fire made two small runs in the area between 1300 and 1600 necessitating the withdrawal of ground forces. Background is a Quick Bird satellite image from Digital Globe taken at 1142 on September 7, 2010.

to reinforce hand-lines constructed by crews when they became available (Figures 37, 40). Multiple drops were also made between 1700 and 1800 west of Gold Hill near the Colorado Mountain Ranch (Figure 41). One Type-1 (i.e., capable of carrying 700 gallons) and one Type-2 (i.e., capable of carrying 300 gallons) helicopters dropped a total of 61,040 gallons of water throughout the fire area. Richardson's Type -2 Incident Management Team assumed command of the fire at 1800.

September 8

On September 8, weather conditions were favorable for fire suppression as the air relative humidity was in the range of 30 percent, light winds were blowing, and 0.08 inches of rain fell at the Sugarloaf RAWS between 1600 and 1700 (Figures 17, 28). Suppression focused on point and structure protection based on fire behavior and public and firefighter safety. Homes within the fire perimeter and those in or nearby subdivisions (e.g., Pinebrook and Boulder Heights) immediately adjacent to the fire perimeter were prioritized for protection. Hand-line construction continued in the Sunshine Saddle area on the northeastern perimeter of the fire (Figure 29).

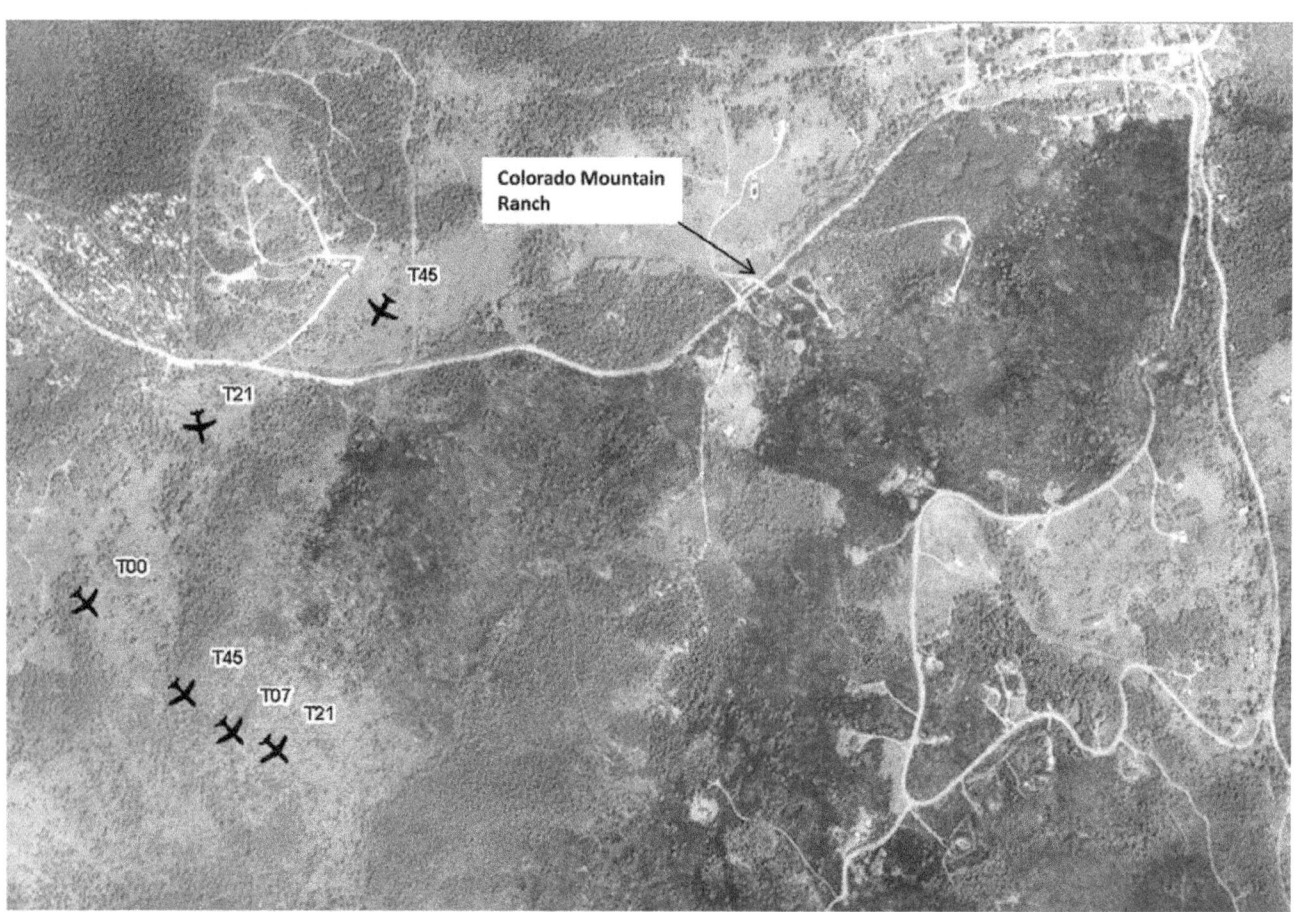

Figure 41. On September 7, 2010, retardant was dropped west of Gold Hill and the Colorado Mountain Ranch. All drops occurred between 1700 and 1800. The background is a Quick Bird satellite image from Digital Globe taken at 1142 on September 7, 2010.

Eight loads of retardant were dropped between 1402 and 1605 in the Boulder Heights area (Figure 42). These drops were adjacent to an area where the fuels had been treated below the housing subdivision; however the fire never reached this area. Three drops (T-10, T-25, T-45) were made to the east of Butzel Hill between 1459 and 1522 (Figure 42) and five drops were made in the Logan Mill area between 1034 and 1125 (Figure 43). Air tanker AT-878 made one and tanker T-48 made five drops on the fire but the drop locations were not recorded. As a result, 22 loads of retardant, equaling 44,741 gallons were dropped on September 8. Additionally, one Type-1 and one Type-2 helicopters dropped a total of 60,840 gallons of water.

September 9

On September 9, suppression focused on points and homes located within and adjacent to the fire perimeter. Hand-line construction continued near Sunshine Saddle and several retardant drops were made in the area (Figures 29, 37). Five retardant drops (11,357 gallons) were made by five tankers in the vicinity of Snowbound Mine, Butzel Hill,

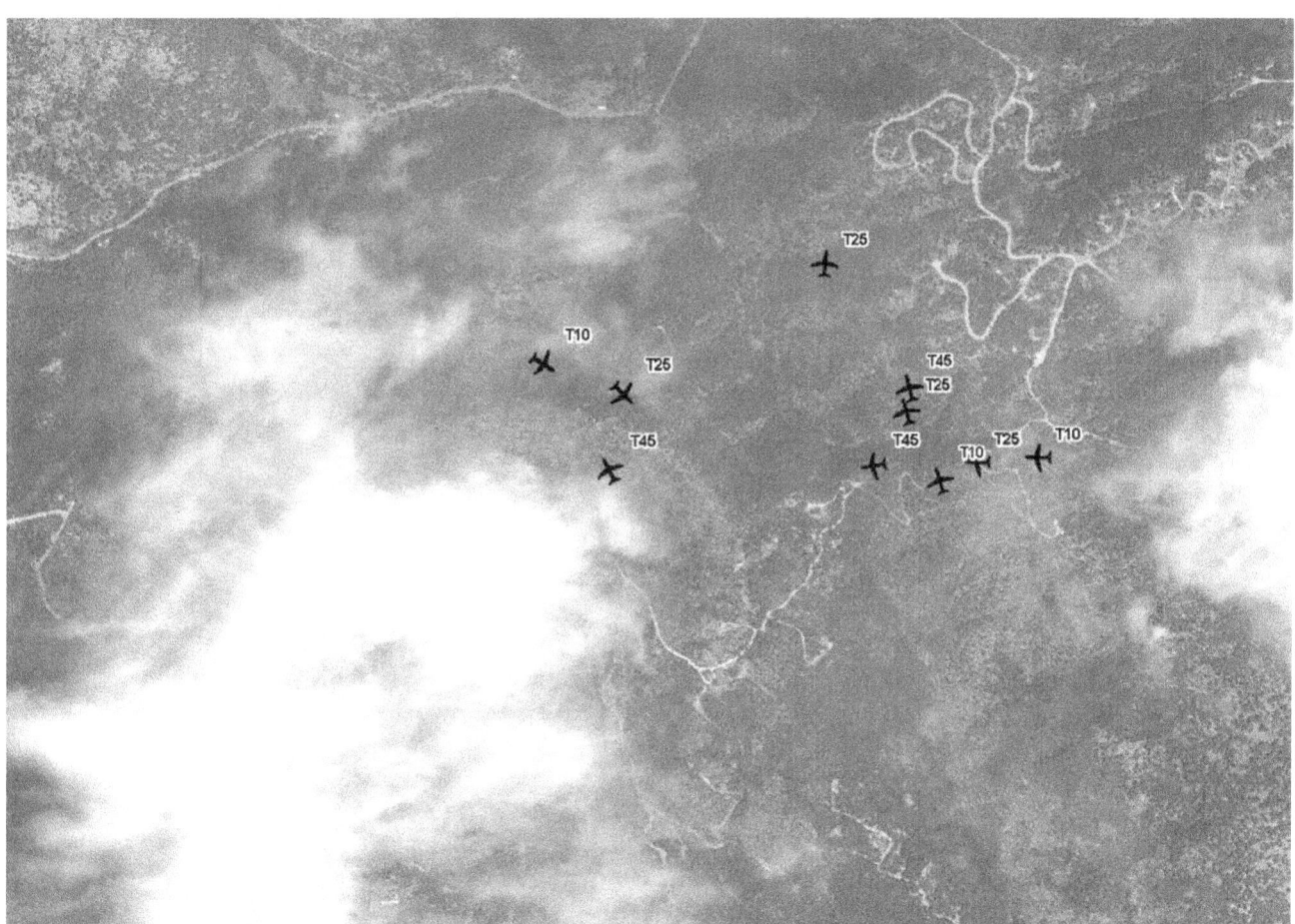

Figure 42. On September 8, seven retardant drops were made adjacent to the Boulder Heights subdivision between 1402 and 1605. Three drops (T-10, T-25, T-45) were made to the east of Butzel Hill between 1459 and 1522. The background is a GeoEye-1 satellite image taken at 1208 on September 8, 2010. Clouds in the image obscure a complete view of the fire area.

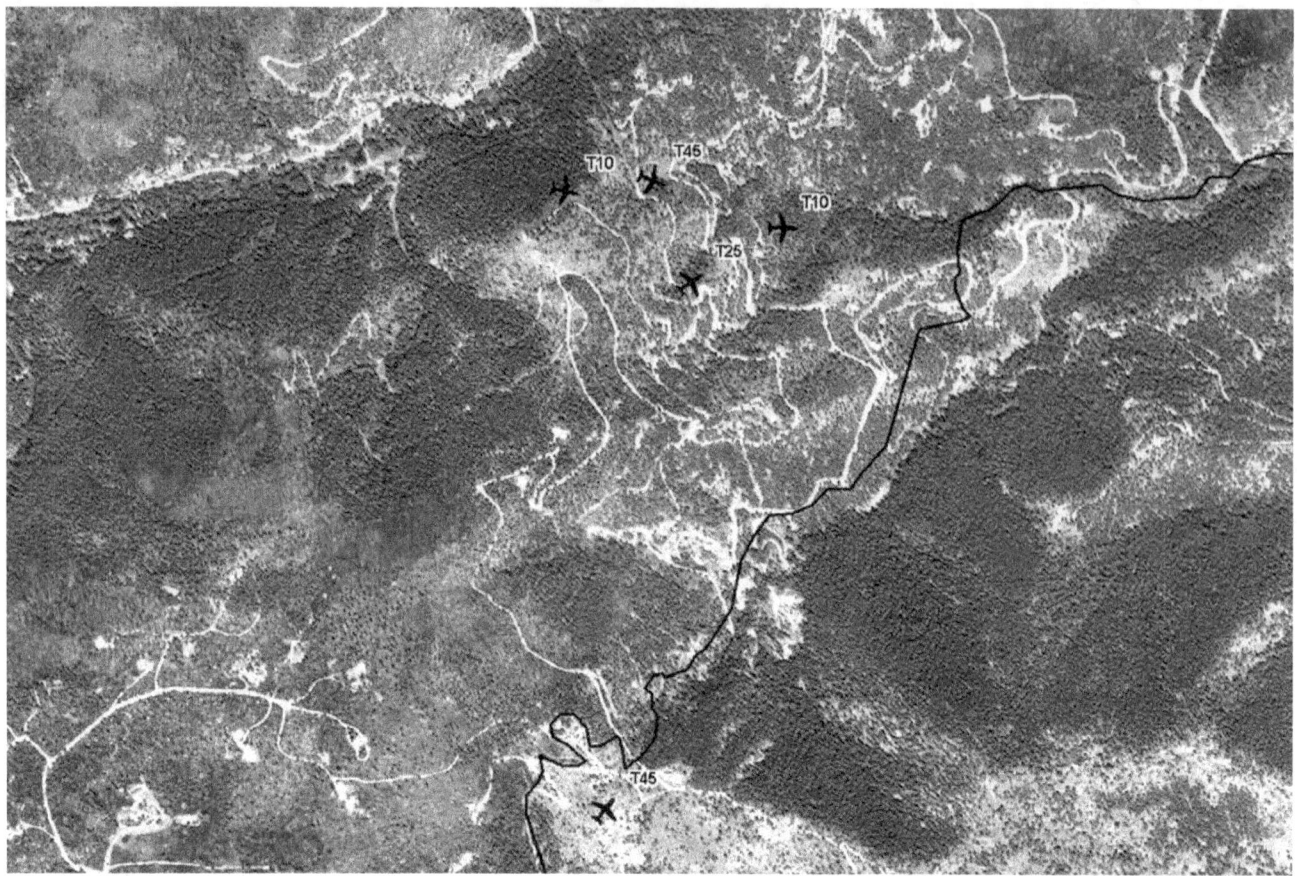

Figure 43. On September 8, several retardant drops were made in the Logan Mill Area. This area was under clouds in available satellite images for September 8, 2010. The background displayed is a GeoEye-1 satellite image from September 10, 2010, at 1142. Red paths in the image are retardant. A total of five drops were made in this area between 1034 and 1125.

and Boulder Heights between 1143 and 1248 (Figure 44). These were the last retardant drops made on the Fourmile Canyon Fire. In addition to the retardant, crews suppressing the fire in this area used a combination of hand-line, check-line, and cold trailing and were supported by helicopter water drops. These and other water drops throughout the fire area made by three Type-1 and one Type-2 helicopters totaled 79,150 gallons.

Thomas's Type-1 IMT assumed command of the fire at 1800 on September 9 as crews were changing. At this time, the wind speeds dramatically increased and the air relative humidity dropped below 20 percent. These weather conditions persisted well into the night increasing the intensity of the fire in many places requiring the shift-length of the day-crews to be extended. The increased fire intensity initiated coordination with the Boulder City Fire Department in the event that the fire advanced towards the City of Boulder. During the night, a spot fire of 2 to 3 acres in size was burning across the containment line near the end of West Coach Road. This fire was contained very early in the morning of September 10.

Figure 44. On September 9, a total of five retardant drops were made in the area of Snowbound Mine, Butzel Hill, and the Boulder Heights subdivision between 1143 and 1248. Background image is a satellite image by GeoEye-1 taken on September 10, 2010, at 1142.

September 10

A Red Flag warning for low air humidity and strong westerly winds until 1800 was issued on September 10. Strong (10 to 13 mph average and 20 to 29 mph gusts) winds were observed at the Sugarloaf RAWS) from 1000 to 1700 and temperatures remained in the 68 to 71 °F range. However, the air relative humidity never dropped below the mid-teens during the day. Suppression priorities remained for point and home protection throughout the fire area. In particular, efforts were made to contain the fire in the Sunshine Saddle area and keep the fire as near to its existing size as possible (Figure 29). A Type-1 helicopter dropped 10,800 gallons of water and a Type-3 (i.e., capable of carrying 4-8 passengers or 100 gallons of water) helicopter flew one reconnaissance flight during the day. By mid-afternoon all air operations were suspended due to the high wind speeds.

USDA Forest Service Gen. Tech. Rep. RMRS-GTR-289. 2012

51

September 11

On September 11 fire suppression focused on the large unburned islands of vegetation within the fire perimeter, which if ignited, would pose a threat to many of the residential areas. Night crews were significantly reduced, consisting mainly of patrols by engines. Three Type-1 and one Type-2 helicopters dropped a total of 51,200 gallons of water.

September 12

Although dry and unstable air (Haines Index of 6) was present over the fire area, minimal flaming occurred or smoke was generated. As a result, no real suppression challenges were presented and no additional perimeter growth occurred. Thomas's IMT was ordered to take on the Reservoir Road Fire, a new start some 12 miles north of the Fourmile Canyon Fire. Numerous ground and air resources were reassigned from the Fourmile Canyon Fire to the Reservoir Road Fire, including the three Type-1 and one Type 2 helicopters. The remaining Type-3 helicopter on the Fourmile Canyon Fire dropped 1,700 gallons of water.

September 13-17

On September 13 suppression focused on locating and extinguishing hot spots and the night shift was reduced to a Division Supervisor and two engines. Suppression focused on completing the mop-up of the fire and the rehabilitation of dozer and hand-lines throughout the fire area. On September 14 the remaining two helicopters dropped the last 8,040 gallons of water throughout the fire area. The fire was declared 100 percent contained at 1800 on September 13 with command of the fire transferred back to a local Type-4 IMT at 0600 on September 17.

Aerial Resources

On the day the Fourmile Canyon Fire started no large air tankers were stationed at the Jeffco Air Tanker Base (Broomfield, Colorado, located ≈20 miles southeast of the fire) and only one SEAT (single engine air tanker, AT-878) was available at Ft. Collins, Colorado (≈40 miles north of the fire). Nevertheless, initial attack personnel inquired about the availability of retardant planes upon arriving at the fire. The SEAT located at Ft. Collins was ordered within 54 minutes of the fire being reported and arrived on the fire at 1158. However, because of the high wind speeds occurring at the fire, it could not safely drop and it jettisoned its load and landed at Jeffco Tanker Base. At 1306 two large air tankers, T-25 located in Grand Junction, Colorado, and T-45 located in Rapid City, South Dakota, were ordered. Upon arriving at the fire, these tankers and the SEAT still could not fly because of the unsafe flying and ineffective retardant application conditions created by the high wind speeds (RMCG 2009, USDA-DOI 2011). On the evening of September 6, the winds shifted (from west to east) and moderated and the two large air tankers (Tankers T-25 and T-45) and one SEAT (AT-878) dropped 25,605 gallons of retardant in the Gold Hill and Bald Mountain areas. Air operations were also suspended on September 10 because of the high wind speeds. From September 6 through 9 a total of 86 loads of retardant totaling 174,149 gallons were dropped from both large air tankers and one SEAT (Table 2). The majority (78.7%) of the total retardant dropped on the fire and 81.3 percent of the total hours the tankers flew occurred on September 7 and 8, after most fire spread had occurred.

52

USDA Forest Service Gen. Tech. Rep. RMRS-GTR-289. 2012

Table 2. The cost of retardant used on the Fourmile Canyon Fire from September 6 through 9, 2010[a].

Date	Tanker number	Type	Retardant cost	Flight cost	Other costs	Total cost	Flight hours	Gallons retardant	Number loads
09/06/10	T25	P3	25,348.00	15,950.52	387.00	41,685.52	2.43	12,674	5
09/06/10	T45	P2V	16,562.00	19,410.57	516.00	36,488.57	3.33	8,281	4
09/06/10	AT878[b]	SEAT	9,300.00	6,994.63	132.00	16,426.63	3.05	4,650	6
Daily total			51,210.00	42,355.72	1,035.00	94,600.72	8.81	25,605	15
09/07/10	T25	P3	30,600.00	23,896.12	516.00	54,012.12	3.38	15,300	6
09/07/10	T45	P2V	30,404.00	26,246.22	516.00	57,166.22	4.18	15,202	7
09/07/10	AT878[b]	SEAT	4,732.50	6,857.03	132.00	11,721.53	2.99	4,575	6
09/07/10	T48	P2V	24,790.00	18,578.25	516.00	43,884.25	3.45	12,395	6
09/07/10	T10	P2V	16,066.00	18,020.73	516.00	34,602.73	2.87	8,033	4
09/07/10	T21	P2V	30,418.00	20,999.40	516.00	51,933.40	3.10	15,209	6
09/07/10	T00	P3	35,192.00	27,299.22	516.00	63,007.22	4.03	17,596	7
09/07/10	T07	P2V	8,272.00	9,920.82	516.00	18,708.82	1.58	4,136	2
Daily total			180,474.50	151,817.79	3,744.00	335,036.29	25.58	92,446	44
09/08/10	T25	P3	25,442.00	12,735.12	172.00	38,349.12	1.88	12,721	5
09/08/10	T45	P2V	20,838.00	15,571.92	172.00	36,581.92	2.48	10,419	5
09/08/10	AT878[b]	SEAT	602.00	1,444.79	176.00	2,222.79	0.63	700	1
09/08/10	T48	P2V	20,864.00	14,162.55	172.00	35,198.55	2.63	10,432	5
09/08/10	T10	P2V	20,802.00	13,311.48	172.00	34,285.48	2.12	10,401	5
09/08/10	T07	P2V	136.00	1,255.80	172.00	1,563.80	0.20	68	1
Daily total			88,684.00	58,481.66	1,036.00	148,201.66	9.94	44,741	22
09/09/10	T25	P3	5,110.00	4,199.88	258.00	9,567.88	0.62	2,555	1
09/09/10	T45	P2V	8,348.00	5,839.47	258.00	14,445.47	0.93	4,174	2
09/09/10	T21	P3	5,100.00	3,590.22	258.00	8,948.22	0.53	2,550	1
09/09/10	T07	P2V	4,156.00	4,269.72	258.00	8,683.72	0.68	2,078	1
Daily total			22,714	17,899.29	1,032.00	41,645.29	2.76	11,357	5
Total			343,082.5	270,554.46	6,847.00	619,483.96	47.09	174,149	86

[a] Information was developed using Daily Cost Summary data from the fire records box and data in the Fourmile Canyon Fire Incident I-Suite archived database. Table does not reflect the total costs for Large Air Tankers on the Fourmile Canyon Fire. Table only shows costs associated with missions of retardant delivery for those days during the fire.

[b] All daily single engine air tanker (SEAT) data was based on invoices obtained from the Colorado State Forest Service. In the incident I-Suite database SEAT entries were combined into a single day entry on 09/09/10 based on the same daily invoices.

Drop locations and the number of individual water drops made by helicopter each day were unavailable. Type-1 (maximum gross takeoff weight, MGTW, greater than 12, 501 lbs.), Type-2 (6,000 to 12,500 lbs. MGTW), and Type-3 (less than 6,000 lbs. MGTW) helicopters were used on the fire beginning on September 7 and worked on the fire through September 15. The majority of flight hours (78.3%) were associated with water drops. These helicopters dropped a total of 272,770 gallons of water with over half the water drops occurring on September 8 and 9 (Table 3). The extensive road network in the area afforded plentiful vehicle access and only 3,400 pounds of cargo and 93 passengers were flown. The passengers were primarily on reconnaissance flights.

Table 3. Costs of helicopters used on the Fourmile Canyon Fire distributed by type from September 7 through 12, 2010[a].

Date	Number	Type	Flight costs	Other costs[b]	Total costs[c]	Flight hours	Water (gal.)[d]	Passengers number	Cargo (lbs)
09/07/10	N173AC	HEL1	58,348.00	0.00	58,348.00	7.90	50,000		
09/07/10	N28HX	HEL2	12,352.00	0.00	12,352.00	6.60	11,040	6	600
09/07/10	N722LM	HEL3	6,412.00	0.00	6,412.00	3.20		6	300
Daily total			77,112.00	0.00	77,112.00	17.7	61,040	12	900
09/08/10	N173AC	HEL1	42,983.00	0.00	42,983.00	5.80	51,000		
09/08/10	N28HX	HEL2	9,438.00	0.00	9,438.00	5.30	9,840	4	600
09/08/10	N722LM	HEL3	4,619.00	0.00	4,619.00	1.70		8	
Daily total			57,040.00	0.00	57,040.00	12.80	60,840	12	600
09/09/10	N173AC	HEL1	40,857.00	0.00	40,857.00	5.50	32,000		
09/09/10	N719HT	HEL1	27,510.00	0.00	27,510.00	3.60	27,600		
09/09/10	N715HT	HEL1	30,917.00	0.00	30,917.00	3.80	12,350		
09/09/10	N28HX	HEL2	7,577.00	0.00	7,577.00	4.20	7,200	2	200
09/09/10	N722LM	HEL3	6,084.00	0.00	6,084.00	3.40		8	
Daily total			112,945.00	0.00	112,945.00	20.50	79,150	10	200
09/10/10	N173AC	HEL1	0.00	1,884.00	1,884.00				
09/10/10	N719HT	HEL1	14,446.00	0.00	14,446.00	1.70	10,800		
09/10/10	N715HT	HEL1	0.00	2,000.00	2,000.00				
09/10/10	N28HX	HEL2	0.00	942.00	942.00				
09/10/10	N722LM	HEL3	0.00	3,843.00	3,843.00	0.80		3	
Daily total			18,289.00	4,826.00	23,115.00	2.50	10,800	3	0
09/11/10	N173AC	HEL1	16,056.00	0.00	16,056.00	2.00	12,000		
09/11/10	N719HT	HEL1	14,940.00	0.00	14,940.00	1.80	10,800		
09/11/10	N715HT	HEL1	26,492.00	0.00	26,492.00	3.40	26,000		
09/11/10	N28HX	HEL2	3,186.00	0.00	3,186.00	1.40	2,400	2	200
09/11/10	N722LM	HEL3	4,360.00	0.00	4,360.00	1.40		6	
Daily total			65,034.00	0.00	65,034.00	10.00	51,200	8	200
09/12/10	N722LM	HEL3	6,062.00	1,175.00	7,237.00	3.20	1,700	8	
Daily total			6,062.00	1,175.00	7,237.00	3.20	1,700	8	0
09/13/10	N28HX	HEL2	2,224.00	0.00	2,224.00	0.80		4	200
09/13/10	N722LM	HEL3	7,785.00	0.00	7,785.00	5.20		10	
Daily total			10,009.00	0.00	10,009.00	6.00	0	14	200
09/14/10	N28HX	HEL2	5,751.00	0.00	5,751.00	3.00	5,040	12	1200
09/14/10	N722LM	HEL3	6,252.00	0.00	6,252.00	3.30	3,000	7	
Daily total			12,003.00	0.00	12,003.00	6.30	8,040	19	1200
09/15/10	N28HX	HEL2	1,357.00	0.00	1,357.00	0.50		5	100
09/15/10	N722LM	HEL3	4,079.00	0.00	4,079.00	0.90		2	
Daily total			5,436.00	0.00	5,436.00	1.40	0	7	100
Total			363,930.00	6,001.00	363,930.00	79.80	272,770	93	3,400

[a] Information developed using Aviation Business System (ABS) records, daily cost summary data from the fire records box and data in the Fourmile Incident I Suite archived database.

[b] Other costs: are costs associated with standby.

[c] Total costs do not include the daily availability rate.

[d] Water delivered should be considered an estimate and is likely low as this entry was often incomplete by individual ship.

Fuel Treatment Efficacy

     Approximately 600 acres of fuel treatments had been performed during the last 7 years within the area ultimately burned by the Fourmile Canyon Fire (Figures 21, 45). However, because of the varied prescriptions used, the intentional leaving of piles of large material in several instances, lack of reducing and maintaining a clean forest floor with the application of prescribed fire, and several areas where the planned treatments were not complete, no general inference can be made on fuel treatment efficacy. In addition, after any fire, little evidence remains of when and how treatment areas were encountered and burned. This creates considerable uncertainty as to the explanations behind what can be observed post-fire. For example, treatment effects can be very different if the fire was heading (with the wind and or slope), flanking, backing down slope, or if the treated area burned as a result of a mass ignition by spotting (Figures 30, 32, 33).

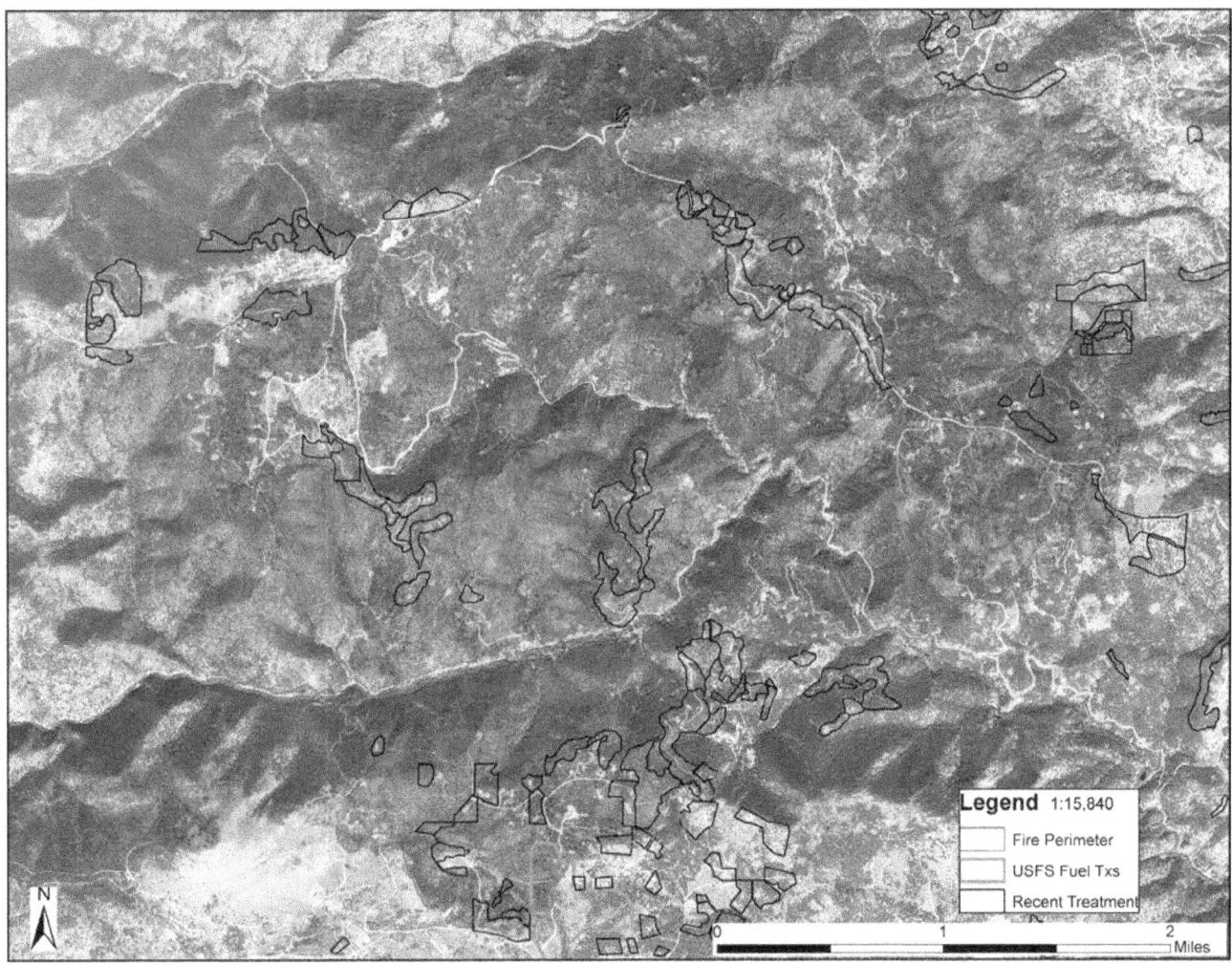

Figure 45. Fuel treatment locations in relation to vegetative burn severity using false color satellite image taken by GeoEye-1 on September 10, 2010, at 1142. The areas shaded in blue are burned or black while the red shaded areas are green or alive. Note that many north facing and predominantly Douglas-fir forests did not burn.

Fuel treatment performance can only be evaluated post-fire based on evidence of changes in fire effects on residual vegetation that can be related to changes in fire behavior and sometimes changes in fire progression. It was clear from photographic evidence that the fire readily burned through the treatments and pervasive spotting (0.5 mi at 1000 and 1.0 mi by 1400 on September 6) during the Fourmile Canyon Fire allowed the fire to easily breach the narrow fuel treatments located throughout the fire area (Figure 21, 45).

No evidence was found that the progression of the Fourmile Canyon Fire was altered by the presence of fuel treatments and the treated areas were probably of limited value to suppression efforts on September 6 (Figure 32). In some cases, because there were large amounts of surface fuels present in the fuel treatments, they appeared to be ineffective in changing fire behavior. Moreover, it was suggested that the large amount of surface fuels present in many of the treated areas was because that they had not been maintained (Boulder Incident Management Team 2010). After September 7 the fuel treatment areas on the eastern perimeter of the fire near Lee Hill and the Church Camp were used by fire crews to access the fire edge. However, the fire never reached these fuel treatment areas and the final fire perimeter was not coincident with the location of the known treatment areas (Figure 45). The changes in fire activity in this area were apparently a result of changing weather (increases in air humidity and decreases in wind speed, see Figure 28) and topography (northerly aspect) rather than any changes in forest structure and composition resulting from a fuel treatment. Several miles of roadside fuel treatments were designed to allow for better driving sight distances along the steep and narrow roads but it was impossible to assess the possible role these treatments had in assisting evacuations (Figures 45, 46).

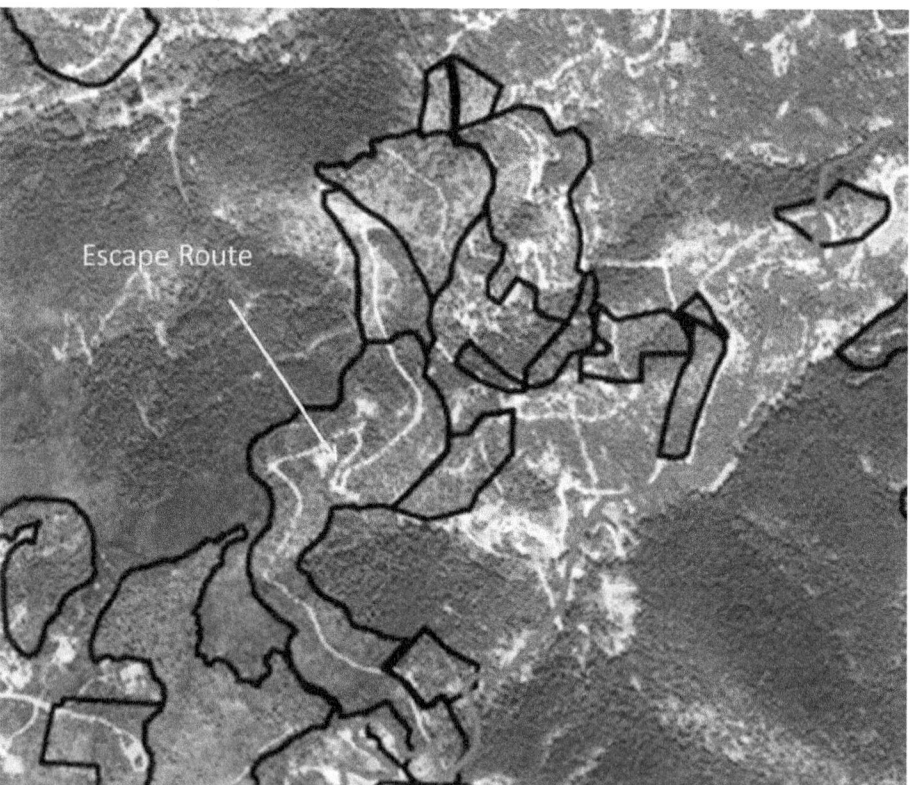

Figure 46. Fuel treatment locations (outlined) in relation to vegetative burn severity using false color satellite image taken by GeoEye-1 on September 10, 2010, at 1142. The areas shaded in blue are burned or black while the red shaded areas are green or have live vegetation. Note the areas where the fuels were treated along the "Escape Route" were burned more severely than neighboring areas where the fuels were not treated.

Post-fire satellite imagery clearly showed the absence of moderated burn severity inside treated areas compared to neighboring untreated stands (Figure 45). In some cases, treated stands appeared to burn more intensely than adjacent untreated stands, perhaps because of additional surface fuels present as a result of the thinning and higher wind speeds that can occur in open forests compared to those with denser canopies (Figure 46). One clear example of this comes from near Gold Hill where the piles of slash were scattered in the understory of a thinned stand but where the intended slash burning had not yet been completed. This situation reinforces the notions that fuel treatment performance metrics should be described and treatments need to be executed as planned to be effective (Figure 47).

The description and documentation of fuel treatments performed in the area where the Fourmile Canyon Fire burned did not mention the weather conditions under which they were intended to be effective nor the methods for maintaining surface fuels (litter, grasses and herbaceous fuels) in a treated condition. The amount and condition of surface fuels present in a forest is the major determinant in fire ignition, spread, and ultimate burn severity (Graham 2003, Graham and others 2004).

Figure 47. In the area near Gold Hill where the fuels had been treated and the slash piles had yet to be burned (yellow outline) fire behavior and intensity were exacerbated (upper left). The intense fire behavior that occurred within the treatment unit was confined to the south facing slope whereas the north facing slope was minimally burned (photo: Greg Cortopassi (upper left); Chad Julien (center)). Background image (upper right) is by the Quickbird satellite from Digital Globe, taken on September 7, 2010, at 1142.

USDA Forest Service Gen. Tech. Rep. RMRS-GTR-289. 2012

57

Although activity fuels (slash or residues from thinning activities) within the Fourmile Canyon Fire were often chipped or piled for later burning, no broadcast prescribed fire was conducted. If low intensity prescribed fires had been applied throughout the area at frequent (e.g., 10 years) intervals, they would have consumed litter layers, killed shrubs and small trees (ladder fuels), and pruned the lower branches of overstory trees by scorching (Graham and others 2004, 2007). By increasing the crown base heights of trees and decreasing surface fuels the occurrence of tree torching may have been reduced (Figure 25).

Based on past studies of treatment performance and under the weather conditions at the time of the fire, the surface fuel conditions in these treatments almost certainly produced high fire intensities and rapid spread rates (Figures 45-47). Even where intensities could have been reduced by the treatments, long duration flaming associated with continuous surface fuels ultimately ignited and torched residual trees (Figure 31). Claims of fuel treatment performance around homes by the owners are consistent with the knowledge that the removal of surface fuel plays an important role in changing fire behavior. Evidence of these effects is seen in the live and minimally scorched tree canopies on their property after a low intensity surface fire most likely burned their property (Figure 48).

Treatment units were located adjacent to roads and on ridge-lines, which confounds treatment effects with those of topographically related changes in fire behavior (Figures 34, 49). Clear evidence of topographic effects is visible in the post-fire burn severity images where north-facing slopes and canyon bottoms suffered minor impacts but had received no treatment (Figures 34, 45). The slim boundary between forest consumed completely by fire and intact north facing forests is coincident with ridgelines and slope changes whether treatments were present or not (Figure 49). Elsewhere, (Gold Hill, Sugarloaf, Bald Mountain, Melvina Road; Figures 45, 47) patterns of burn severity (living and consumed conifer foliage) were found to vary independently of fuel treatment locations (Figures 29, 45). Therefore, it is impossible to distinguish the various causes of burn severity, including the efficacy of the fuel treatments.

High wind speeds and the low relative humidity of the air during the Fourmile Canyon Fire are common weather conditions associated with large wildfires along the Front Range foothills (Figure 2). Thus, recognizing these conditions is critical when developing fuel treatment prescriptions. By doing so, and appropriately designing fuel treatments (treating surface fuels, ladder fuels, and canopy fuels in this order of importance) in and among landscapes in conjunction with treating fuels in the Home Ignition Zone across the Front Range, the efficacy of fuel treatments can be greatly improved (Figure 20) (Graham and others 1999, Graham 2003, Graham and others 2004, Graham and others 2009, Hudak and others 2011).

58

USDA Forest Service Gen. Tech. Rep. RMRS-GTR-289. 2012

Figure 48. An example of a homeowner treating both canopy and surface fuels around their home that resulted in low burn severity to the vegetation. Note the low burn severity resulting from a surface fire to the left of the home even as an intense fire approached the home as shown in the top photo (photos: Dave Steinmann (middle and bottom); Mary Alston (top)).

USDA Forest Service Gen. Tech. Rep. RMRS-GTR-289. 2012

59

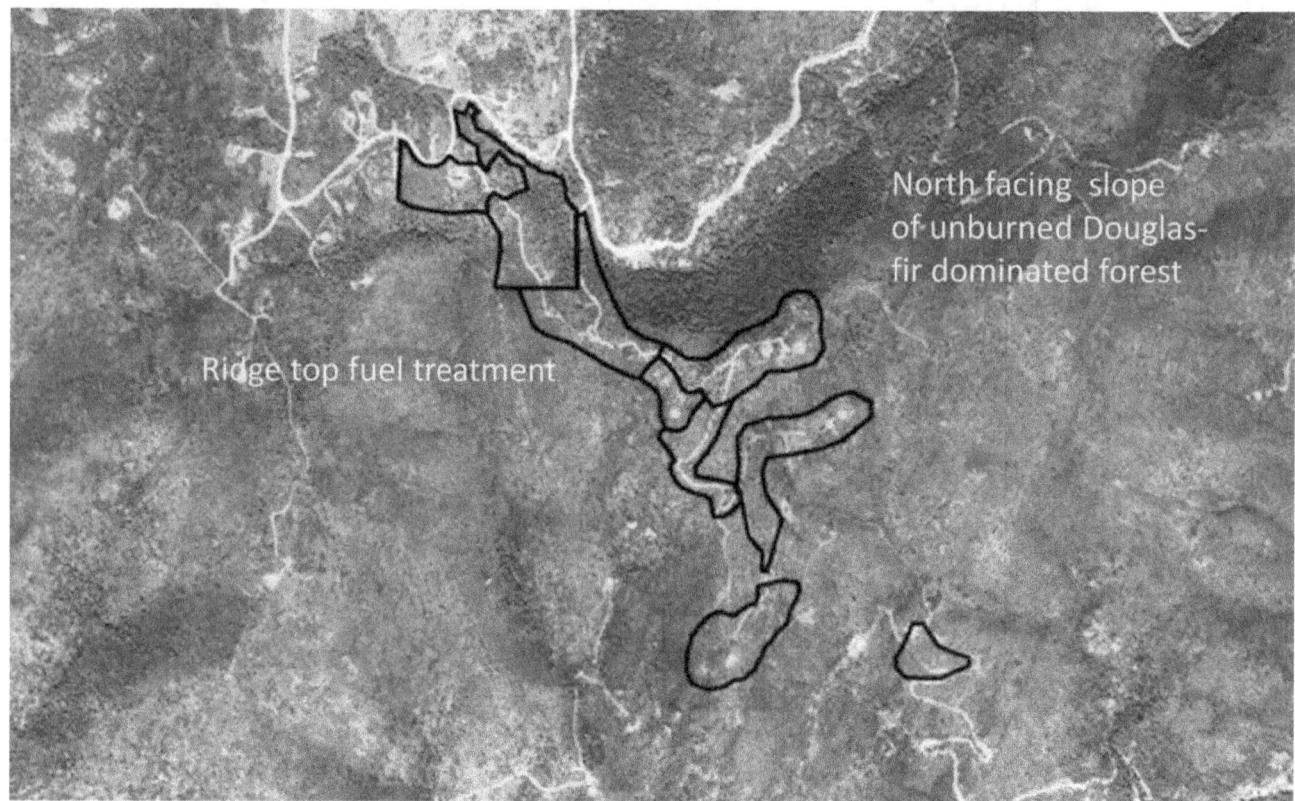

Figure 49. When fuel treatments were located along the ridge tops the efficacy of the fuel treatment in modifying fire behavior and/or burn severity is confounded by the change in topography and in this case vegetation. The areas shaded in blue are burned or black while the red shaded areas are green or alive. Note that north facing and predominantly Douglas-fir forest did not burn next to where the fuels were treated. The background is a false color satellite image taken by GeoEye-1 on September 10, 2010, at 1142.

Home Destruction

Residential Wildfire Results

The threat to and destruction of residential development by fire in wildland vegetation has become known as the wildland urban interface (WUI) fire problem. A total of 474 homes were within the final perimeter of the Fourmile Canyon Fire or within 100 feet of the perimeter (Figure 50). We assumed these homes to be significantly exposed to wildfire flames and/or firebrands (e.g., wind carried burning twigs, needles) and of that total residential wildfire exposure the following resulted:

- 168 (35%) of the total homes within or adjacent to the fire perimeter were destroyed;
- 29 homes (17% of destroyed homes) were destroyed associated with crown fire;
- 139 homes (83% of destroyed homes) were destroyed associated with surface fire; and
- 162 homes were destroyed within the first 12 hours the fire burned.

High fire spread rates (i.e., 0.5 to 1.0 mph) and long-distant (i.e., 0.5 to 1.0 miles) spotting combined to produce rapid wildfire growth rates accompanied by high intensity burning (Figures 30, 32). Areas of high wildfire intensities tended to occur on upper slopes and ridges with lower fire intensities in canyon and valley bottoms (Figure 34).

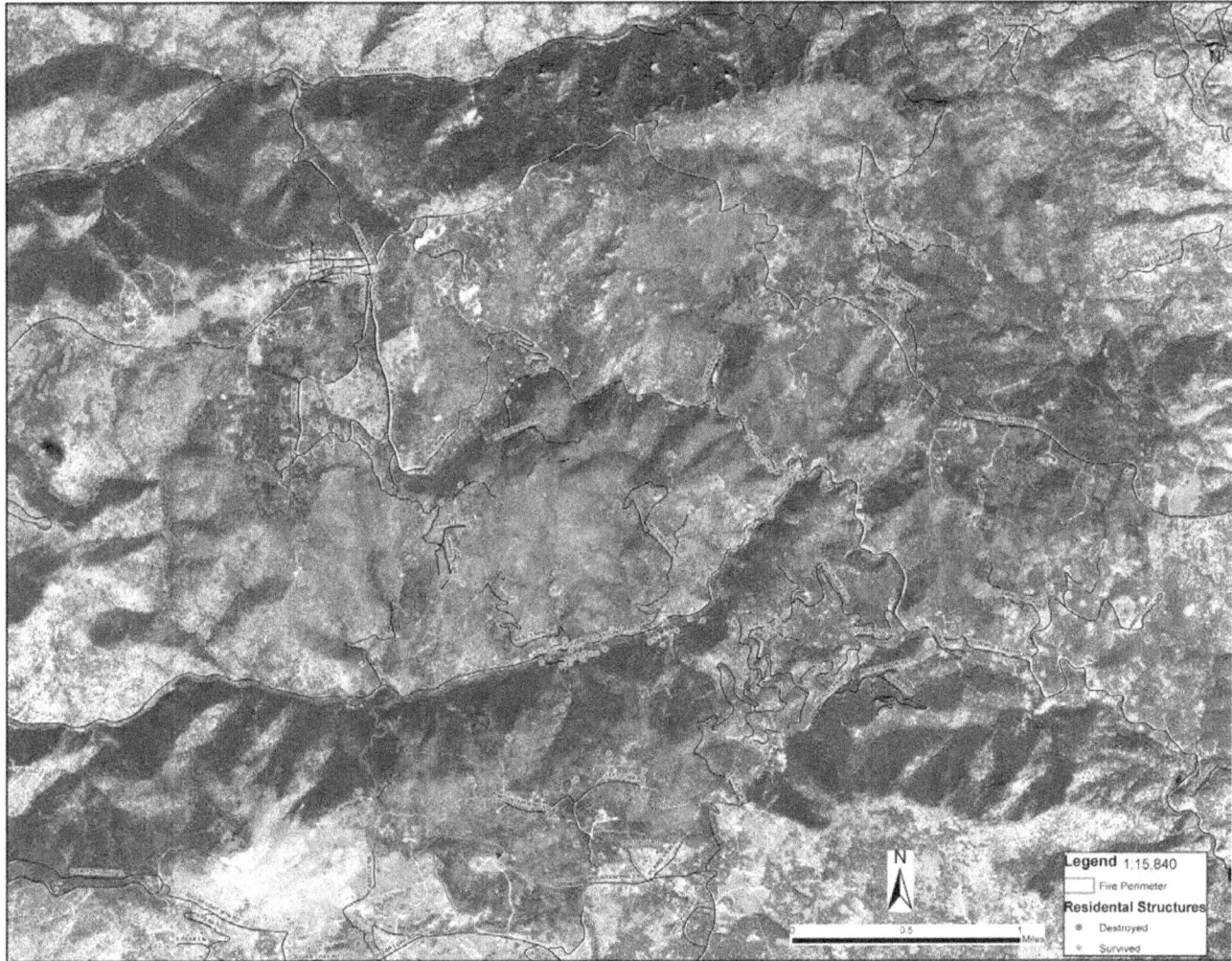

Figure 50. Destroyed and surviving homes in the area where Fourmile Canyon Fire burned are displayed on a true color satellite image taken by GeoEye-1 on September 10, 2010, at 1142.

Especially on September 6, the extreme burning conditions overwhelmed wildfire suppression efforts. Because of the rapid growth rate, wildfire quickly spread to the widely dispersed residential areas resulting in hundreds of homes being exposed to potential ignition in a brief period of time. Wide ranging flame and firebrand exposures resulted in simultaneous home ignitions that overwhelmed structure fire protection capabilities. House-to-house fire spread did not occur, largely due to significant spacing between homes (relatively low home density). In addition, the rate of structure fire involvement after ignition was slow compared to wildfire spread. Homes were typically burning well after the wildfire had passed and thus burning structures did not significantly contribute to wildfire growth. The Fourmile Canyon Fire home destruction scenario followed the same pattern as other WUI fire disasters that have occurred in the United States. This pattern of residential destruction, largely unique to WUI fires, is shown by the sequence in Figure 51.

WUI Disaster Sequence

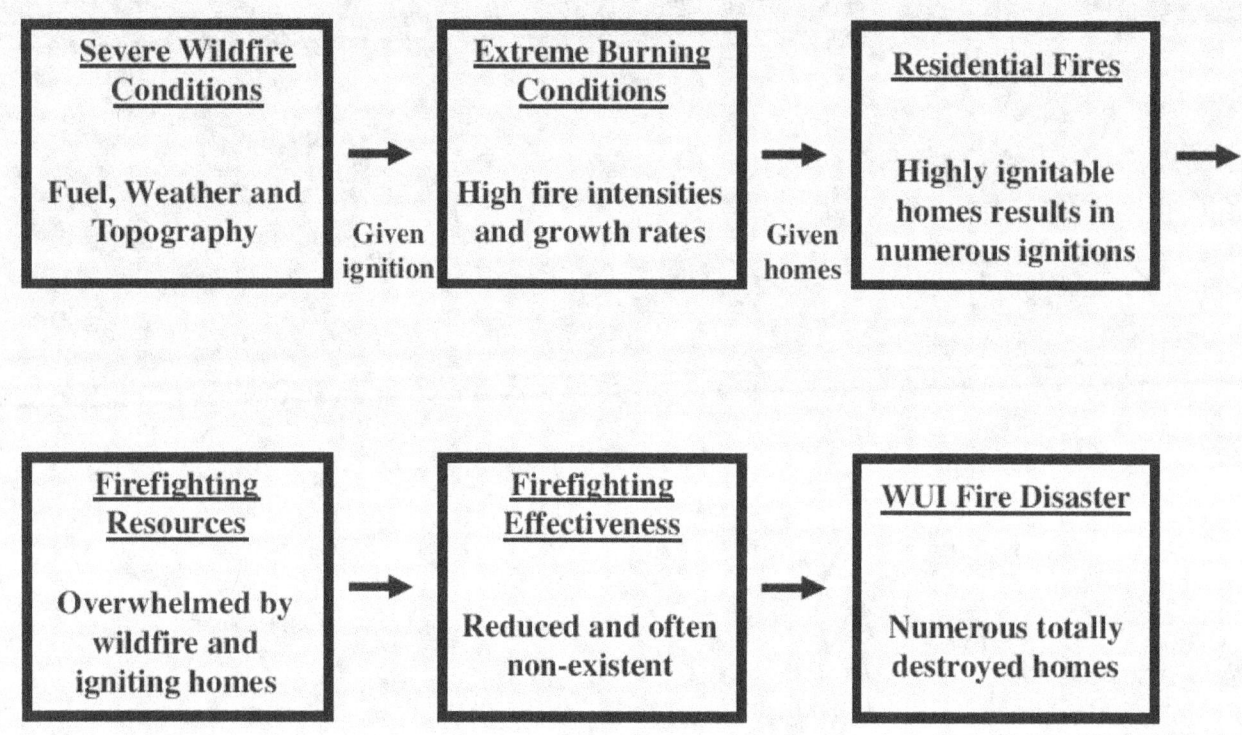

Figure 51. The wildland urban interface (WUI) disaster sequence begins with overwhelming wildfire conditions simultaneously igniting numerous homes. Hundreds to thousands of homes exposed to flames and firebrands overwhelm structure protection. Note, however, that WUI fire disasters depend on highly ignitable homes (upper right box). If ignition resistant homes do not ignite, then firefighters can effectively protect homes. As a result, the wildfire occurs without disastrous residential destruction.

The overwhelmed structure fire protection capability during the Fourmile Canyon Fire is revealed by comparing the available firefighting resources at the end of the first burning period on September 6 (39 engines, 12 water tenders, 150 personnel; Figure 52) with the estimated total number of exposed homes (474) and destroyed homes (162) during that period. If there had been no life safety limitations (not realistic) and we assume two firefighters per house, nearly 85 percent of the exposed homes could not have been protected from the initial wildfire exposure. Furthermore, there were more than nine homes for each engine and water tender at the end of the primary period of house exposure. Given the general necessity of water tenders for structure fire protection and assuming all engines and crews were structure fire capable, only a few simultaneously burning homes exhausted all available structure fire resources.

USDA Forest Service Gen. Tech. Rep. RMRS-GTR-289. 2012

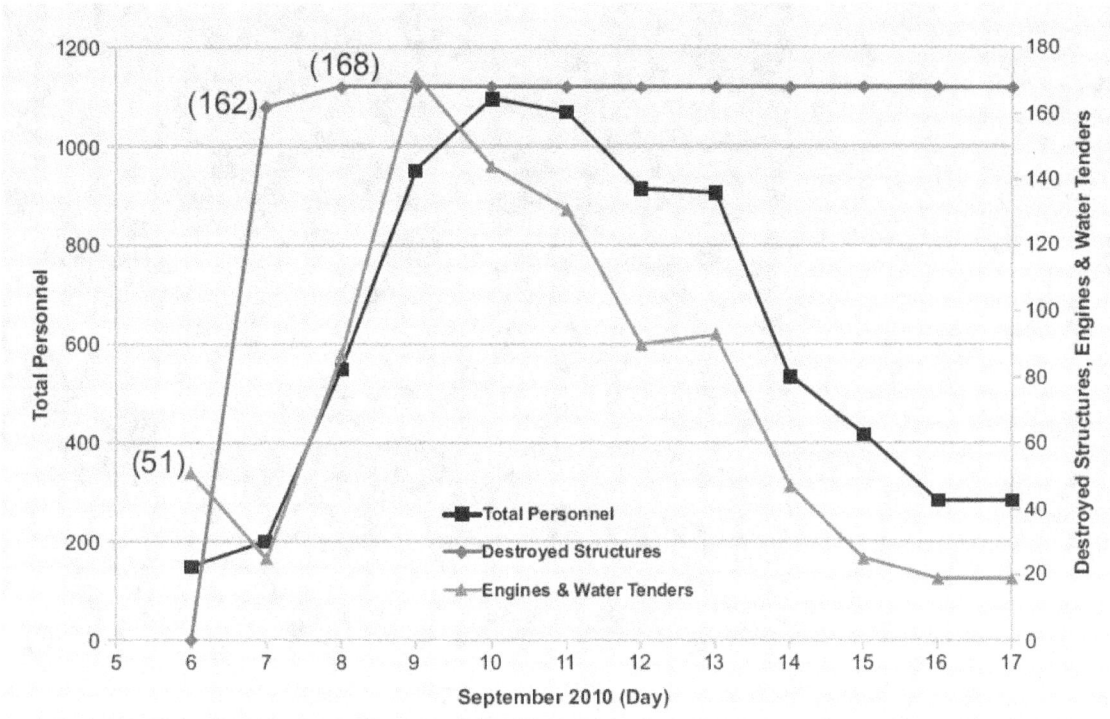

Figure 52. The estimated available firefighting resources at the end of September 6 were 51 engines and water tenders and 150 personnel. This is compared to an estimated 162 destroyed homes. Given highly ignitable homes, available firefighting resources were minimally capable of protecting all the affected residential areas by the end of September 9.

This scenario does not suggest the solution to the WUI fire problem is having more engines; it illustrates that extreme WUI fire conditions overwhelm generally capable wildfire suppression and structure protection capabilities. The Fourmile Canyon Fire situation is comparable to the findings of previously examined home destruction associated with extreme wildfire behavior conditions—rapid spread rates and high intensities (e.g., Black Tiger (NFPA 1989), Painted Cave (Foote 1994), Spokane '91 (NFPA 1992), Los Alamos (Cohen 2000a), Hayman (Cohen and Stratton 2003), Grass Valley (Cohen and Stratton 2008).

With most residents evacuated and firefighters unable to protect most homes, unprotected homes incurring sustained ignitions freely burned to total destruction. Thus, the total destruction of homes is not indicative of high fire intensity or massive flame fronts engulfing a home. Any sustained ignition from whatever source resulted in total home destruction. For example, home destruction associated with low fire intensities are revealed as varying degrees of unconsumed vegetation and other flammable materials adjacent to a totally destroyed home (Figure 53). This corresponds to the overwhelmed fire protection leading to total home destruction displayed in Figure 51. During the Fourmile Canyon Fire, most homes with sustained ignitions freely burned to total destruction due to no one extinguishing initial burning.

The Fourmile Canyon Fire home destruction was similar to previous WUI fire disasters in other aspects as well. In other WUI fires, most of the home destruction occurred during relatively brief episodes of extreme burning conditions with some homes burning afterward (Cohen and Stratton 2003, 2008). Even with fire protection overwhelmed,

Figure 53. An example of total home destruction surrounded by unconsumed vegetation indicates the ignition was associated with a low intensity fire exposure (photo: Boulder County Sherriff Office).

nearly two-thirds (65 percent) of the exposed homes survived the Fourmile Canyon Fire. During the fire, most of the 168 destroyed homes burned within the first 12 hours (est. 162 homes). In the following 2 days, burning within or near the final wildfire perimeter resulted in the estimated destruction of six more homes (Figure 52).

Home Destruction

Homes ignite and burn during wildfires when the *requirements for combustion*, a sufficiency of fuel, heat and oxygen, are sustained at one or more places on a home. If the requirements for combustion are not met, homes do not ignite and thus, do not burn. If homes do not burn during a wildfire then the WUI fire disaster does not occur. This is evident from the disaster sequence shown in Figure 51; a rapidly spreading, high intensity wildfire can occur but without home ignitions a WUI fire disaster does not occur. In the context of WUI fire disasters, a home is the fuel and all things burning around the home (including other structures) provide the heat (Figure 54).

The Fourmile Canyon Fire is a specific case of home destruction during extreme wildfire burning conditions. However, we can generally define WUI fire destruction in terms of the requirements for combustion (Butler 1974).

WUI fire destruction occurs when the wildfire spreads from wildland fuels to residential fuels. For this to occur the wildfire must be close enough for its lofted firebrands and/or flames (sufficient heat) to ignite the flammable parts (sufficient fuel) of a home.

We can conceptually describe home ignition during wildfires as a conditional probability. That is, the probability that a home's ignitable materials (structure and debris) will ignite conditional on some level of wildfire exposure from flames and/or firebrands. Regardless of the general wildfire behavior, the resulting home survival or destruction without protection always depends on the site-specific flame and firebrand home exposures in relation to the availability of flammable materials (structure and debris)

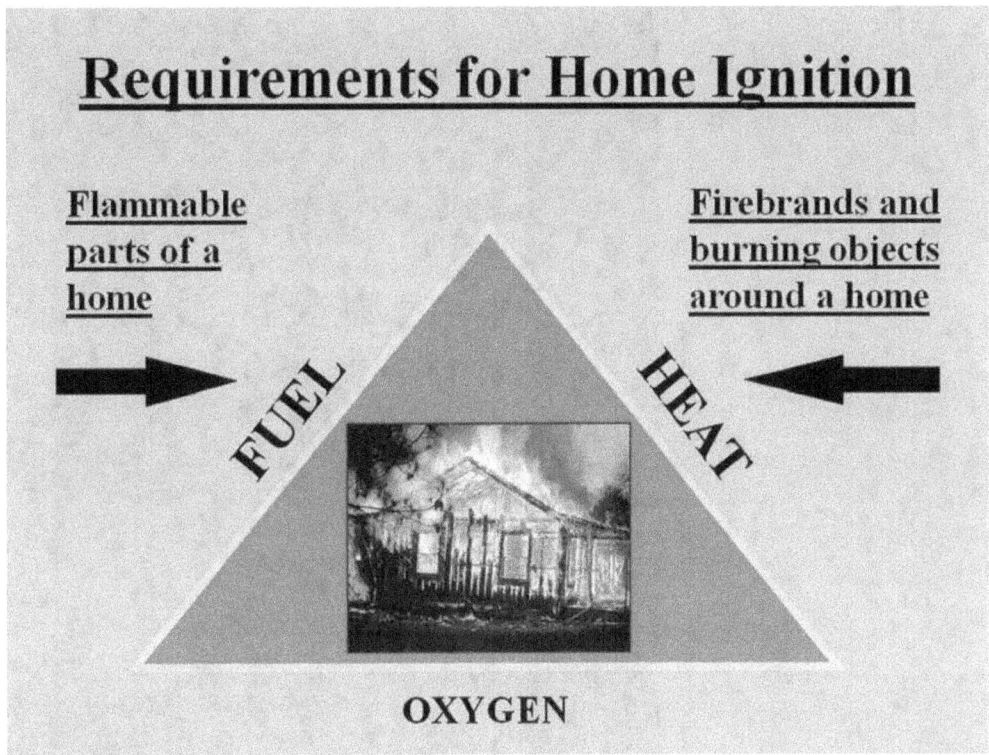

Requirements for Home Ignition

Flammable parts of a home

Firebrands and burning objects around a home

FUEL

HEAT

OXYGEN

Figure 54. Homes sustain ignition by meeting the requirements for combustion—a sufficiency of fuel (home), heat (burning objects around a home), and oxygen (which is always sufficient). Home ignitions do not require massive flame fronts to burn through residential areas; firebrands accumulating on flammable surfaces and low intensity surface fire contacting a wood wall can be sufficient.

to sustain home ignitions. Determining how a home is destroyed or survives requires explicit, site specific information of the flame and firebrand exposures, home ignition vulnerabilities, and in the case of home survival, any protection actions that occurred. In addition, an understanding of how the requirements for combustion are met during a WUI fire is prerequisite to examining how home destruction occurs during wildfires and ultimately how to reduce WUI home ignition potential.

Existing research on how residential fire disasters occur and how homes ignite during wildfires indicates that given extreme burning conditions, home characteristics in relation to a home's immediate surroundings (100 ft) principally determine home ignition potential (Howard and others 1973, Foote 1994, Cohen 1995, Cohen 2000a, 2000b; Cohen and Stratton 2003, Cohen 2004, Cohen and Stratton 2008, Cohen 2008). The area of the home and its immediate surroundings is called the *home ignition zone* (HIZ). Commonly home ignition occurs over small distances—a few tens of feet or less. During extreme burning conditions such as crown fires, the flames outside the HIZ (beyond 100 ft) will not ignite a home's combustible materials. Fires spreading into and firebrand ignited fires within the HIZ must be closer than 100 feet and/or contact the flammable parts (e.g., shake roof, wood siding, wood deck) of a home before direct flame ignition occurs. Home ignitions from firebrands require lofted burning embers from whatever distance and source (e.g., burning vegetation and/or structures) to accumulate on a home's flammable materials (e.g., litter covered roof, decorative bark, ornamental shrubs) before ignitions can occur. Figure 55 shows a home from the Fourmile Canyon Fire area that had an ignition resistant HIZ and the home survived.

USDA Forest Service Gen. Tech. Rep. RMRS-GTR-289. 2012

65

Figure 55. This is an example of a home ignition zone (HIZ) and how it reduces ignition potential within 100 feet of a home. Home construction was nonflammable or ignition resistant. Areas adjacent to the home were irrigated plantings or nonflammable materials. Firebrands landing on and around the home had few flammables to ignite. Surface fires were not eliminated within the HIZ but importantly, were restricted by the landscaping design from burning to contact the home. Trees that would produce high intensities were separated, thereby reducing the chances of canopy burning and, when not prevented, the burning canopies produced significantly less radiant heating to the home (photo: Joe Amon).

Inspection of the example HIZ in Figure 55 indicates firebrands landing on and around the home had few flammables to ignite. Note that surface fires were not eliminated within the HIZ but were restricted by the landscaping design from spreading to contact the home. Trees that would produce high fire intensities when burning had sufficient canopy separation to eliminate the potential for crown fire spread. In addition, when tree torching did occur, the separated burning canopies produced significantly less radiant heating to the home than they would have if the tree canopies simultaneously burned (Cohen and Butler 1998).

The concepts of home ignition potential and the HIZ provide a basis for better understanding how some homes can survive and others burn within areas of high and low intensity wildfire (Figure 56). We expect home destruction due to high intensity exposures (close proximity crown fire) and survival with low intensity (or no) fires spreading near a home. But past examinations (Cohen 2000a, Cohen and Stratton 2003, Cohen and Stratton 2008) indicate home destruction mostly occurs with low and moderate intensity burning near homes. Commonly high intensity canopy fires cease their spread within residential areas. WUI fire examinations indicate roads, driveways, utility corridors and home sites themselves break the vegetation continuity thereby disrupting high intensity shrub and tree canopy fire spread. However, surface fires continue and firebrands are lofted downwind to ignite fires within the residential area. This was evidenced in the Fourmile Canyon Fire and helps explain how we found 83 percent (139/168) of the Fourmile Canyon Fire home destruction was not directly associated with intense wildfire.

House Exposure-Results Matrix

Figure 56. Home destruction and survival are associated with both high and low intensity fire exposures. Most destroyed homes (139, 83%) in the Fourmile Canyon Fire occurred with low fire intensities in the home ignition zone (HIZ) (photo: Dave Zader (upper left); Joe Amon (all others)).

Using the HIZ and requirements for combustion as analysis guides, we generally examined home destruction and survival related to wildfire flame exposure. We estimated wildfire flame exposure (high or low intensity fires) based on the degree of consumed vegetation and other flammables surrounding a home. Consistent with home ignition potential as determined by the limited area of the HIZ, we found home survival within areas of complete vegetative destruction, destroyed homes in areas with variable vegetative burn severity, and, commonly, homes destroyed surrounded by unconsumed, green vegetation (Figures 53, 56, 57).

Figure 57. Top photo shows surviving homes (O) with destroyed neighbors (X) (photo: Dave Zader). The middle photo shows destroyed homes (O) with surviving neighbors (photo: Joe Amon). The bottom photo shows a destroyed home with adjacent green vegetation (photo: Boulder County Sherriff Office).

Our examination only related home destruction to a categorical estimate of flame intensity as described in the previous paragraph (Figure 56). Home destruction and survival was the result of a home's specific flame and firebrand exposures in conjunction with its flammable materials (e.g., siding, roof) and debris (e.g., grasses, shrubs, decorative bark). Because explicit ignition exposures to all home flammables were unknown we could not reliably determine specific causes for destruction or survival. Thus, we could not specifically relate the general data on building materials and defensible space/fuel treatments to home destruction and survival. Also, we categorically described home destruction with greater reliability than home survival. For total home destruction, fire protection was clearly not effective and could be eliminated as a factor; however, the varying degree and effectiveness of fire protection could not be reliably described in most cases of home survival.

Key Elements for Preventing WUI Fire Disasters

Home ignition potential is principally determined by the HIZ and has profound implications for preventing future WUI fire disasters. Moreover, minimizing home ignition potential enhances life safety and firefighter effectiveness especially during extreme burning conditions. Given the inevitability of future wildfires and extreme burning conditions that overwhelm fire protection, focusing on reducing home ignition potential is the key to preventing WUI fire disasters. Reducing the availability of home fuels in relation to potential firebrand exposures and reducing the surrounding heat sources in the HIZ can significantly reduce home ignition potential.

- Residential fire protection effectiveness and enhanced life safety during extreme burning conditions depend on the HIZ conditions producing low home ignition potential.
- The HIZ is largely owned by the homeowner or homeowners in higher density residential development. That means the responsibility for reducing vulnerability to wildfire rests with the homeowner(s). Thus, WUI fire disasters cannot be prevented without homeowners actively creating and maintaining HIZs with low home ignition potential.
- Given the inevitability of wildfires on the Colorado Front Range, we have the opportunity to significantly reduce the potential for WUI fire disasters during extreme burning conditions. However, this opportunity requires a change of approach—an approach focused on reducing home ignition potential within the HIZ rather than increasing expensive fire protection capabilities that have proven to strategically fail during extreme wildfire burning conditions.

Social/Economic _____

Fire Management Costs

Total fire management (suppression, emergency management, and post fire rehabilitation) is estimated at $14.1 million; however, total fire costs have not been finalized. The State of Colorado estimates total suppression cost for the Fourmile Canyon Fire to be $10.1 million. Cost breakdowns by day and resource type are available from the I-Suite database maintained by the incident command teams during the fire. The I-Suite database accounts for $9,959,068 in suppression expenditures between September 6 and September 16, 2010. It is not unexpected that the reported final fire cost may differ from those listed in I-Suite for several reasons, including charges billed after September 16, 2010.

USDA Forest Service Gen. Tech. Rep. RMRS-GTR-289. 2012

69

Daily cost, and cost by resource category are available in Table 4 and Figure 58. Over the duration of the fire the largest cost component was for engines representing 30 percent of total cost ($2,975,766). This was not surprising given the number of homes within the fire perimeter and the extent of the point protection (e.g., protecting specific homes, structures etc.) mission. Aviation costs represented 15 percent of total fire cost ($1,508,529) of which approximately 9 percent of total cost ($892,272) was spent on retardant drops from large air tankers. We estimated that 93 percent of the area burned in the first day of the fire while only 6 percent of the suppression costs were incurred the first day. A total of 20 percent of all suppression expenditures were made in the first 2 days of the fire (September 6 and 7). The value of the suppression investment after the initial fire run was in reducing loss from future fire spread and home protection that may have prevented additional home loss. However, the potential for the fire to expand beyond the established perimeter in absence of suppression was not assessed.

An established Cost Share Agreement identifies final suppression cost responsibility by partner. Costs were distributed based on early estimates of proportion of jurisdiction within the final fire perimeter. The agreement has Boulder County, through the State of Colorado Emergency Fire Fund, responsible for 67 percent (FEMA Category H Federal Wildfire Assistance Grants will cover 75 percent of approved costs), Bureau of Land Management (BLM) 28 percent, and U. S. Forest Service (USFS) 5 percent—BLM and USFS typically do not reconcile costs as per established interagency agreements. Table 5 presents suppression costs itemized by partner prior to redistribution of funds. Costs are based on the Cost Share Agreement and updated assessment of area burned by partner showing that Federal Lands constitute 28 percent not the 33 percent as estimated with the cost share agreement.

Final suppression cost was $1,634 per acre. The U.S. Forest Service and Department of the Interior utilize a regression based cost model (Stratified Cost Index (SCI)) for performance reporting to Congress (Gebert and others 2007). The SCI is based on ignition characteristics, and coarse proxies of values at risk. At a cost of $1,634 per acre, the fire cost falls within the 75 percent zone; the fire was more expensive than 75 percent of fires with similar ignition characteristics. Given the very high level of private values at risk and associated losses, higher than average costs are not unexpected. Additionally, the fire was primarily a Colorado State fire, whereas the SCI is based on fires managed by the U.S. Forest Service.

Boulder County spent $492,104 on non-suppression related emergency management (such as road blocks, evacuations, sheltering animals, etc.) that was partially covered under FEMA Fire Management Assistance Grant Program, Category B, Emergency Protective Measures. FEMA has reimbursed the County for 75 percent ($369,078) of these costs with an additional reimbursement of donated services of $79,592 (this reimbursement cannot exceed 25 percent of Category B expenditures). Total cost under these categories, including donated services, was $571,696.

Boulder County reports a total of $3.4 million in external grants received for rehabilitation and recovery of the burned lands. Of this $2.2 million was from federal sources with the State of Colorado contributing the remaining $1.2 million. The recovery grant for Fourmile Emergency Stabilization was funded at $2.7 million (federal: $2.2 million, State: $500,000) with BLM treatments estimated at $1.07 million. In the initial emergency stabilization report, mulching treatments were estimated to represent a majority of total costs. Asbestos debris removal was estimated at $500,000.

70

USDA Forest Service Gen. Tech. Rep. RMRS-GTR-289. 2012

Table 4. Costs of suppressing the Fourmile Canyon Fire distributed by suppression activity from September 6 through 16, 2010.

	9/6/2010	9/7/2010	9/8/2010	9/9/2010	9/10/2010	9/11/2010	9/12/2010	9/13/2010	9/14/2010	9/15/2010	9/16/2010
Air Tanker	$211,474	$328,601	$151,134	$182,124	$17,133	$1,806	$0		$0	$0	$0
Aviation(tot)	$221,018	$453,732	$266,371	$317,908	$58,647	$86,898	$27,550	$30,007	$20,090	$15,779	$10,529
Engines	$223,511	$446,172	$423,607	$385,376	$358,075	$368,680	$276,070	$206,371	$121,279	$86,706	$79,919
Direct	$519,822	$1,145,048	$1,052,208	$1,126,669	$846,181	$845,246	$656,585	$513,352	$264,002	$176,073	$154,245
Support	$57,402	$230,414	$291,497	$428,022	$368,087	$312,397	$276,753	$261,308	$229,866	$139,903	$63,988
Total	$577,224	$1,375,462	$1,343,705	$1,554,691	$1,214,268	$1,157,643	$933,338	$774,660	$493,868	$315,976	$218,233

USDA Forest Service Gen. Tech. Rep. RMRS-GTR-289. 2012

71

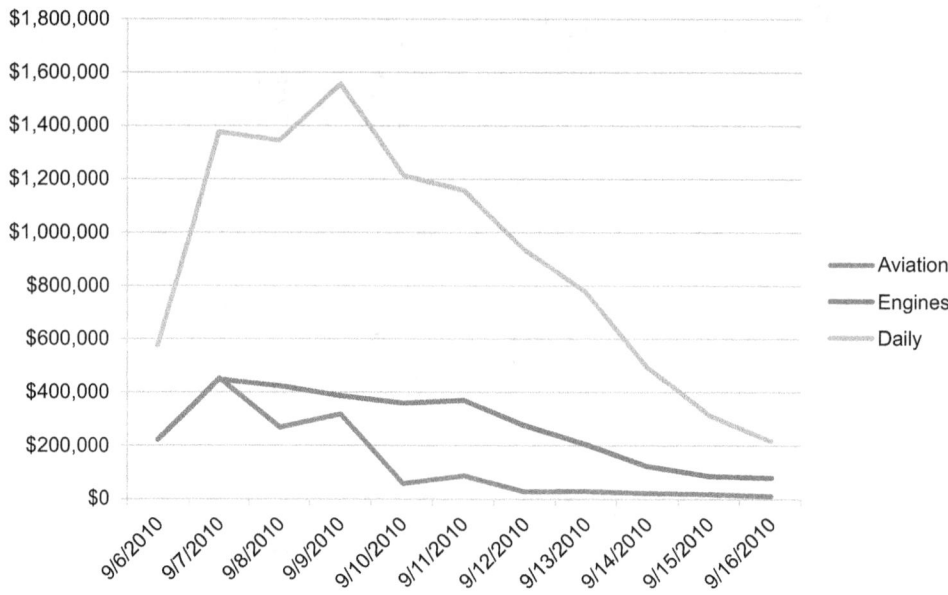

Figure 58. Daily suppression costs for the Fourmile Canyon Fire peaked on September 9.

Table 5. Suppression expenditures incurred by the different agencies responsible for the Four-mile Canyon Fire[a].

Agency	2010 expenditures	Acres	Percentage acres	Percentage cost
Federal expenditures				
BIA	$14,758	0	0	0.1
FWS	$24,453	0	0	0.2
NPA	$79,620	0	0	0.8
BLM	$494,836	1397	22.6	5.0
USFS	$3,316,837	306	5.0	33.3
Total Federal	$3,930,503	1703	27.6	39.5
State and County	$6,028,565	4478	72.4	60.5
Fire total	$9,959,068	6181	100.0	100.0

[a] The Cost Share Agreement established during the fire event lists cost responsibilities for all suppression costs, including aircraft, outside of mutual aid as: Boulder County - 67 %; Bureau of Land Management - 28 %; USFS - Arapaho Roosevelt NF - 5 %.

USDA Forest Service Gen. Tech. Rep. RMRS-GTR-289. 2012

Economic Losses

Economic losses were primarily associated with the loss of private property. The Rocky Mountain Insurance Information Association (RMIIA) provided a final estimate of insured losses of $220 million (personal communications with Carole Walker RMIIA September 28, 2011). Indirect economic costs such as homeowner displacement, disruption of economic activity, and recreation value loss were not estimated due to the complexity of estimating these costs. Additionally, we do not have any information on potential smoke related health issues stemming from the fire.

The Boulder County Assessor's Office reported that total taxable property loss exceeded $125 million (personal communications Rex Westen, Senior Residential Appraiser). Tax loss to Boulder County in 2011 equaled $822,852, with 2010 tax loss equal to $51,045 (partial year adjustment for lost structures; land value could not be adjusted). Lost tax revenue in 2012 and beyond is dependent on the number of homes rebuilt and the recovery of the characteristics of the properties. The Boulder County Assessor's office has an established property appraisal process for subsequent years. The value of building contents lost (both insured and uninsured) and the cost associated with displacement and relocation were not estimated. However, many homeowners appear to be underinsured (see insurance discussion below). A follow up survey of homeowners who either had their homes damaged or destroyed suggested that over half were underinsured and the average estimated cost to replace and or repair minus insurance was $195,000.

Research suggests that significant reduction in home sale price, adjacent, but not within the perimeter of large wildfires can occur. For example, 5 years after the Buffalo Creek fire near Pine, Colorado, in May of 1996, there was a $17,100 to $18,500 (15% to 16%) loss in median home value relative to expected sale prices if there had been no fire (Loomis 2004). Similarly, wildfires in northwest Montana have had a dramatic effect on home sale prices suggesting sale prices of homes within 3 miles of a wildfire burned area were 12.7 percent ($33,053) lower than equivalent homes at least 12 miles from a fire. Sale prices of homes between 3 and 6 miles from a wildfire burned area were 7.3 percent ($18,884) lower than equivalent homes at least 12 miles from a fire (Stettler and others 2010). However, there is anecdotal evidence that residential sales in areas proximate to Fourmile Canyon Fire were active following the fire with a number of residents who lost their homes in the fire choosing to purchase homes in the vicinity of the fire instead of rebuilding (personal communication, Rex Westen- Senior Residential Appraiser, Boulder County Assessor's Office June 28, 2011).

Social Attitudes

Numerous damaging wildfires have occurred in Colorado since 1976, several of which occurred along the Front Range. Firefighters have been killed and 100s of homes destroyed within the hundreds of thousands of acres burned (Table 1). These fires provide the context for the attitudes of the people living in and near where the Fourmile Canyon Fire burned. Post-fire surveys of residents were not administered due to time constraints associated with federal survey approval requirements through the Office of Management and Budget. However, surveys had been conducted of WUI residents within Larimer and Boulder Counties in 2007 regarding wildfire risk perceptions and mitigation efforts. Of the respondents within the original survey, 127 were within areas evacuated during the Fourmile Canyon Fire. The evacuees' perceptions of wildfire risk and what specific actions residents had taken to mitigate the risk within the evacuated area were ascertained for this subsample (Brenkert-Smith and Champ 2011).

Overall survey respondents were fairly familiar with wildfire, with 83 percent reporting being somewhat or very aware of wildfire risk when they bought their current residence and 61 percent had experienced a wildfire within 10 miles of their property.

USDA Forest Service Gen. Tech. Rep. RMRS-GTR-289. 2012

73

A high proportion (83%) of respondents knew someone who was evacuated due to wildfire and 38 percent knew someone whose residence was lost or damaged due to a wildfire. Within the survey area it appears that many residents had conducted some level of mitigation work on their property. Only 4 percent of the survey respondents reported not taking any of the actions. Within the survey, residents were queried on 12 different types of mitigation efforts. On average, Fourmile Canyon Fire respondents implemented 6.52 measures. The mitigation effort with the highest level of participation (72%) was removing dead or overhanging branches within 30 foot perimeter of the home. Installing fire resistant siding and installing screening over roof vents were the two activities with the lowest reported frequencies.

A critical finding was that despite their relatively high familiarity with wildfire, most respondents did not believe that characteristics of their structure and the immediate surroundings of the structure were significant factors influencing the likelihood of a wildfire damaging their property within the next 5 years. Specifically, only 20 percent of respondents believed that vegetation on their own property and only 9 percent believed that the physical characteristics of the house were major contributors to the chances of wildfire damaging their property.

Fuel Treatment Costs

From a basic economic standpoint the appropriate way to view the effectiveness of fuel treatments is at the programmatic level using expected value change. Fuel treatments are effectively risk mitigation efforts and should be designed such that the economic benefits of the entire program in terms of reduced expected loss due to treatments plus any ancillary benefits, such as improved tree vigor and aesthetics, exceed the total cost at the programmatic level. The specific characteristics under which the treatments will interact with fire are unknown at the time of treatment design. However, we do know the conditions under which economic losses typically occur in the Front Range of Colorado: rapid large fire spread under extreme fire weather conditions (high fire danger, i.e., high energy release component and high winds). Therefore, it is critical that treatments be designed to affect change to wildfires under those conditions where loss typically occurs. Further, since it is unknown when and where fires will burn when treatments are designed and the amount of area burned is a small percentage of the entire landscape, most areas receiving fuel treatment will never interact with wildfire. Therefore, the realized benefits (i.e. reduced losses) from treated areas that interact with wildfire should be counted against the cost of all treatments within the area covered under the program.

A substantial amount of fuel treatments had occurred within and adjacent to the final fire perimeter since 2002. We estimated that a total of 600 acres of fuel treatments occurred within the fire perimeter. Most of these treatments were coordinated through the Colorado State Forest Service (CSFS) fuel treatment grant program. Associating total cost of treatments that were engaged by the fire is difficult due to the fact that many projects were split between areas within and approximate to the fire perimeter and areas beyond the perimeter. Additionally, there were three significant treatments: one U.S. Forest Service treatment and two treatments completed by Boulder County Parks and Open Space. A total of 74 projects totaling 823 acres coordinated by CSFS were within one-half mile of or contained within the final fire perimeter. Within the final fire perimeter, 417 spatially located acres were treated of which 113 acres were on Bureau of Land Management (BLM) lands with treatments administered by CSFS under the Good Neighbor Authority (GAO 2009). An additional 162 non-located acres were treated and tended to be defensible space projects surrounding individual homes. Within the fire perimeter, 21 acres were treated by the U.S. Forest Service and 2.5 acres were treated by Boulder County Parks and Open Space.

Fuel treatment costs covered under the CSFS grant process within and adjacent to the fire perimeter totaled $1.175 million. Of this total, grant funding provided $506,000, Bureau of Land Management funded $94,000, and awardee matching provided $576,000. This resulted in a cost per acre of $1,430 ($1,577 adjusted to 2010 dollars). Past research on fuel treatments in Colorado showed treatment costs ranging between $840 and $1,330 per acre adjusted to 2010 dollars (Lynch and Mackes 2003). Thus these treatment costs appear to be on the higher end than past averages, although the small size of treatment units may explain the difference. Two treatments adjacent to the fire perimeter were conducted by Boulder County Parks and Open Space in 2007 and 2008. The Bald Mountain project treated a total of 50 acres at a cost of $118,000 or $2,350 per acre (2.5 acres of the treatment were spatially identified within the fire perimeter). The Gold Hill project treated 12.5 acres at a cost of $59,800 or $4,784 per acre. The U.S. Forest Service conducted a 100-acre fuel treatment in 2005 with 21 acres contained within the final fire perimeter. U.S. Forest Service costs were estimated at $480 per acre and excluded any planning costs associated with the project.

Strategic Wildfire Risk Management

A conceptual model of wildfire management allows us to consider the major drivers of and strategic options for mitigating wildfire risk (Figure 59). Strategic prevention efforts can reduce the number of wildfires and associated damage from human caused ignition. Given an ignition in the absence of suppression, fuels, weather, and topography drive wildfire behavior. Of these, only fuel conditions can be meaningfully modified, and proactive fuel management seeks to alter the quantity, structure, and continuity of fuels so as to induce desirable changes in fire behavior and/or burn severity (Agee and Skinner 2005). Suppression activities generally seek to inhibit or prevent the growth of active wildfires, reducing the likelihood that the fire will engage important values. Collectively these factors influence wildfire extent and intensity, which in turn determine

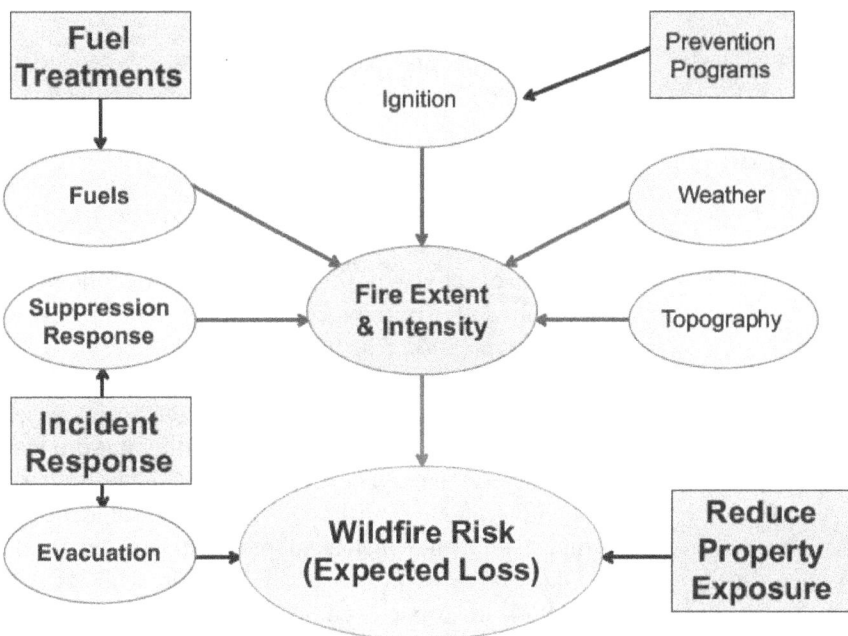

Figure 59. A conceptual diagram of wildfire risk assessment adopted from Calkin and others (2011). The major drivers of fire extent and intensity are represented as ovals, and the major strategic options for mitigating risk are represented as rectangles.

the consequences (detrimental and beneficial) to human and ecological values. A last strategic option is to not focus on wildfire occurrence or fire behavior directly, but rather to lessen the consequences of an interaction with fire, which, in this framework, can be accomplished in two ways. First, emergency response teams can address the first priority of fire management, human health and safety, by administering residential evacuation once a fire has occurred. Second, proactive mitigation of the home ignition zone (HIZ) and use of fire-resistant materials in home construction can reduce the likelihood of structure damage or loss.

Using this framework we can evaluate how existing mitigation efforts performed relative to their intent as well as establish strategic objectives moving forward that could efficiently reduce wildfire risk in the Colorado Front Range. Strategic objectives for mitigation efforts focus on reducing the likelihood, extent, and/or intensity of the hazardous event or reducing the effects if the value of concern (e.g., social, ecological, property) is exposed to hazard. We can also define appropriate strategic objectives for mitigation programs that were engaged by the Fourmile Canyon Fire.

Fire Prevention

Although the Fourmile Canyon Fire was human caused, we will not evaluate the costs and benefits of prevention programs since this report focuses on characteristics of the fire that did occur. Research has been conducted in the Southeastern United States that suggests prevention education programs have a high return on investment (Prestemon and others 2010). Following the Fourmile Canyon Fire, Boulder County has initiated several wildfire education programs promoted by the Citizen Advisory Team of the Boulder County Community Wildfire Protection Plan. The team has developed several recommendations and is in various stages of implementation. In October 2011 Boulder County initiated Wildfire Awareness Month including numerous community events and associated presentations. Partners included fire protection districts, private businesses, the Colorado State Forest Service, the U.S. Forest Service, the City of Boulder, the University of Colorado, the Boulder County Sheriff's Office, and the Boulder County Land Use and Parks and Open Space Departments. In so doing, it appears that Boulder County and the interested parties have a good foundation for continued development of and implementation of fire prevention activities.

Incident Response

Incident response can be separated into two categories: wildfire suppression response, and emergency response. As stated above, "suppression" attempts to inhibit or prevent the growth of active wildfires, reducing the likelihood that the fire will engage important values. Given the burning conditions of the first day, when a majority of the fire area burned, suppression response was not able to substantially alter fire growth, although targeted efforts likely prevented some structure loss during the fire. Once the wind speeds decreased and the relative humidity of the air increased and fire behavior moderated, fire suppression was effective in containing the fire in a relatively short time period.

Alternately, "emergency management" attempts to protect residential life and safety through evacuation from the wildfire's path. Boulder County had made substantial investments in emergency management coordinated by the Sheriff's Department. Following the Olde Stage Fire in January of 2009, the County realized the existing organizational framework and capacity could not deal with extended attack and, therefore, authorized the formation of a Type-3 Incident Command Team in June of 2009. The adoption of Incident Command System principles and the fact that Sheriff's Deputies had assigned vehicles, thus reducing response time to the fire, facilitated the evacuation of over 3,000 residents with no loss of life or injury to residents or response team personnel. The

Boulder County Emergency Management System is conducted in a new state of the art Emergency Operations Center (EOC) built in 2008. The EOC coordinated communication, provided resource and operational support and information management. Further, Boulder County has adopted the After Action Review process for both the Type-3 Incident Management Team and the Emergency Management System identifying successes and challenges encountered during the fire to facilitate learning and process improvement. It is important to recognize that despite the potential threat to residents and responders posed by the Fourmile Canyon Fire, the emergency response facilitated an extensive evacuation effort with no injury or loss of life during the fire. Similar to being proactive in fire prevention Boulder County sets the standard for their emergency preparedness to wildfires and, for that matter, all crises.

Fuels Management

From a basic economic standpoint, the most concise strategic objective for a fuel treatment program is to reduce expected value loss under the wildfire conditions where loss occurs. This can be accomplished by reducing fire spread and/or intensity and allowing suppression resources to be effective. For a fuel treatment to function effectively it must first spatially interact with an actual wildfire, and second mitigate fire behavior according to design objectives (Syphard and others 2011). Fuel treatments are effectively risk mitigation efforts and should be designed such that the economic benefits of the entire program in terms of reduced expected loss due to treatments plus any ancillary benefits, such as improved tree vigor and aesthetics, exceed the total cost at the programmatic level. The specific characteristics under which the treatments will interact with fire are unknown at the time of treatment design. However, we know the conditions under which substantial economic losses typically occur in the Front Range of Colorado: rapid large fire spread under extreme fire weather conditions (high fire danger, low air relative humidity, and high winds). Since it is unknown when and where fires will burn when treatments are designed and the amount of area burned is a small percentage of the entire landscape, most areas receiving fuel treatment will never interact with wildfire. Therefore, the realized benefits (i.e. reduced losses) from treated areas that interact with wildfire should be counted against the cost of all treatments within the area covered under the program. Within the Fourmile Canyon Fire perimeter, evidence of reduced fire extent and intensity due to treatment was not apparent and the ability of suppression response to utilize existing treatments to stop fire spread was not clearly documented. This review suggests that strategic fuel planning and implementation, especially surface fuel management, is needed on the Front Range. By doing so, the effectiveness of fuel treatments to produce desired outcomes under the weather conditions experienced during the Fourmile Canyon Fire would be more likely.

Home Ignition Zone

Mitigation of the home ignition zone (HIZ) and the use of fire-resistant material in home construction can reduce the likelihood of structure damage or destruction if a fire occurs. Additionally, it may provide a location of safe refuge if a fire occurs and evacuation routes are impeded. As noted previously, most residents within the Fourmile Canyon Fire evacuation area had conducted some level of mitigation to their property. However, under the burning conditions exhibited the first day, when most of the homes were destroyed, sufficient structure protection was not available to protect every home threatened. Therefore, the mitigation efforts necessary for a home to survive in the absence of protection resources is considerably higher than if resources are present. Given the occurrence of rapidly spreading wildfires on the Front Range and the potential of limited structure protection resources relative to homes engaged by a wildfire, mitigation

USDA Forest Service Gen. Tech. Rep. RMRS-GTR-289. 2012

77

efforts within the home ignition zone may need to be designed such that the structure can survive without protection. Not only is this need evident where the Fourmile Canyon Fire burned but throughout the Front Range and, for that matter, wherever wildland urban interface lands may occur.

Summary _____

The Fourmile Canyon Fire occurred just west of Boulder, Colorado, along the Front Range of the Rocky Mountains where the prairie meets the forests. These mixed ponderosa pine and Douglas-fir forests tend to be relatively open and dominated by the pine on south facing slopes and more closed and fir dominated on the north facing slopes. Grasses, shrubs, and small trees, along with a dense layer of ponderosa pine needles, made up the forest floor and ground-level vegetation on the rugged and steep slopes dotted with many homes. Narrow, winding, and steep roads offered access to much of the area as a result of the mining legacy dating back to the 1870s. With this setting on September 6, 2010, some 6 miles west of Boulder, Colorado, an emergency 911 call reported a fire in Emerson Gulch near where it intersects with Fourmile Canyon, not too far from the old Wall Street mill site. Within minutes of the fire report at 1002, the Fourmile Canyon Fire was on its way to being one of the most damaging in Colorado's history.

Weather

- The spring and summer of 2010 along the Front Range were cooler and wetter than normal.
- By late August a very dry weather pattern emerged.
- No vegetative killing frost had occurred by September 6.
- Fire danger expressed as Energy Release Component (ERC) of the National Fire Danger Rating System was at a record level for early September.
- On September 5 near record high temperatures were recorded all along the Front Range. A dry cold front passing on the night of September 5 resulted in gusty winds but minimal increases in the air relative humidity during the night.
- On September 6, gusty westerly winds, not unusual along the Front Range, blew steadily at Sugarloaf RAWS from 0700 to 1800 with sustained winds averaging about 12 miles per hour and gusts mostly ranging from 20 to 30 miles per hour.
- At 1000, a sustained westerly wind of 15 mph with a gust of 41 miles per hour was recorded. Both of these values exceed the 99th percentile for the general fire season at Sugarloaf RAWS.
- At 1000 the temperature was down 19 degrees F from 24 hours earlier, but the relative humidity of the air was only 3 percent lower than 24 hours before and 28 percent lower than just 4 hours earlier at 0600. Air relative humidity dropped to 7 percent and remained below 10 percent until 1800.
- Highly impacted by the steep and complex topography, strong surface winds were blowing in all directions.
- The prolonged period of exceptionally low air relative humidity and windy conditions during the first day of the fire were major contributors to the fire's rapid spread rate (0.5 to 1.0 mph) and high intensity burning.

78

USDA Forest Service Gen. Tech. Rep. RMRS-GTR-289. 2012

Fire Behavior

- Surface fire dominated the fire behavior, but tree torching often occurred and crown fires burned many dense stands.
- At ignition, the fine dead fuels (grasses, needles, etc.) had a moisture concentration of 5 percent.
- At 1002 when the fire was reported, the probability of ignition from firebrands was estimated to be 55 percent and rose to 90 percent by 1700 as fine dead fuel moisture concentrations dropped to less than 2 percent.
- When reported at 1002 the fire was starting spot fires over 0.5 mile ahead of the flaming front and the surface fires were spreading at over 0.5 miles per hour.
- Most fire growth (93% of the area burned) was over by 2000 on September 6 with the last burning occurring near the Lee Hill antenna site.

Fuel Treatments

- The treated areas were small and narrow. They ranged from less-than 1 acre to 52 acres in size and only 4 units were greater than 20 acres in size.
- No performance metrics were defined for the fuel treatments. In other words, the environmental conditions in which the treatments were to be effective in modifying fire behavior or burn severity were not defined.
- Thinning trees to a specified density (residual basal area) or spacing was the prescription often negotiated with land owners. In addition, the treatments were often focused on improving the health of the forest (removing diseased and malformed trees, i.e., dwarf mistletoe) rather than designed to modify fire behavior if a fire was to occur.
- High wind speeds and low air humidity during the Fourmile Canyon Fire are common weather conditions associated with all large wildfires along the Front Range and, thus, should be accounted for in any fuel treatment prescription.
- Pervasive spotting observed during the Fourmile Canyon Fire easily breached the narrow fuel treatment units and rendered them of limited value to suppression efforts.
- The abundance of grasses, forbs, shrubs, and often branches and twigs that could have been removed through judicious surface treatments (e.g., prescribed fire) occurred within the areas where the fuels had been treated and contributed to the high fire intensities and rapid fire spread rate observed.
- Post-fire satellite imagery clearly showed the absence of moderated burn severity inside treated areas compared to neighboring untreated stands. In some cases, treated stands appeared to burn more intensely than adjacent untreated stands, perhaps because of additional surface fuels present as a result of the thinning. One clear example of this comes from near Gold Hill where the piles of slash were scattered in the understory of a thinned stand where the intended burning had not yet been completed.
- Claims of fuel treatment performance around homes by the owners are consistent with the knowledge that additional attention to surface fuel removal plays an important role in changing fire behavior. Evidence of these effects is seen in the generally green tree canopies occurring on their property.
- Treatment units were located adjacent to roads and ridges, which confounded treatment effects with those related to topographic and/or vegetative changes.

USDA Forest Service Gen. Tech. Rep. RMRS-GTR-289. 2012

79

Suppression

- At time of ignition and throughout the first day, a consolidated suppression effort focusing on perimeter control of the fire was not established. This was because the fire was rapidly spreading in multiple directions (north towards Gold Hill, to the south towards Sugarloaf and to the east down Fourmile canyon above Wall Street) and later towards Sunshine Canyon Road. The overall emphasis was placed on life safety, evacuations, point protection when and where safely feasible, and the control, status, and assignment of incoming resources.
- At ignition, the high wind speeds prohibited the use of any air tankers until 1700 on September 6. Likewise, because of the windy conditions, no helicopters were used on the first day.
- In the evening of September 6 when the winds shifted and moderated, two large air tankers and one single engine air tanker (SEAT) dropped 25,605 gallons of retardant in the Gold Hill and Bald Mountain areas. A total of 86 loads of retardant totaling 174,149 gallons were dropped from both large air tankers and one SEAT from September 6 through 9. On September 7 and 8, 78.4 percent the total retardant used on the fire was dropped.
- Type -1, -2, and -3 helicopters were used on the fire beginning on September 7 through September 15. These helicopters dropped 272,770 gallons of water. Because of the extensive road network in the area only 3,400 pounds of cargo and 93 passengers were flown. The passengers were primarily on reconnaissance flights.

Home Destruction

- A total of 474 homes were located within and adjacent (~ 100 feet) to the final wildfire perimeter.
- 168 or 35 percent of the homes within the burned area were destroyed during the Fourmile Canyon Fire. This is within the percentage range of homes destroyed in other wildland urban interface (WUI) fire disasters.
- Within the Fourmile Canyon Fire
  - 29 destroyed homes were associated with crown fire.
  - 139 destroyed homes were associated with surface fire
  - 162 homes were destroyed within the first 12 hours.
  - The initial rapid fire growth and intense burning overwhelmed fire suppression and structure fire protection capabilities.
- The low housing density did not result in house-to-house fire spread; the slow rate of home fire involvement and burning compared to wildfire spread did not enhance overall wildfire behavior/intensities.
- Eighty-three percent of home destruction did not directly result from exposures to surrounding high intensity crown fire and this is consistent with other WUI fire disasters. Although exact ignition causes are not known, without high intensity exposures, home destruction must be due to direct firebrand ignitions and/or surface fire spreading to contact the home.
- Exact causes of home ignitions and exact exposures to flames and firebrands are, with rare exception, unknown during WUI fires. Thus, the effectiveness of specific vegetation treatments and structure materials cannot be determined from WUI fire analyses.
- Survival or destruction of homes exposed to wildfire flames and firebrands (lofted burning embers) is not determined by the overall fire behavior or distance of firebrand lofting but rather, the condition of the Home Ignition Zone (HIZ)—the design, materials and maintenance of the home in relation to its immediate surroundings within 100 feet.

- Society has the opportunity to significantly reduce the potential for WUI fire disasters during extreme burning conditions such as the Fourmile Canyon Fire, but this opportunity depends on homeowners creating and maintaining low home ignition potential within the HIZ. Reducing wildfire home ignition potential is predicated on the home having ignition resistant materials and the homeowner removing flammable debris from on and around the house and maintaining this condition. If flammable vegetation is not continuous (landscaping, driveway, etc.) to the home, firebrand ignited spot fires cannot spread to and contact the home. Additionally, if trees within 100 feet of a home are not continuous or are deciduous the potential for active crown fire is minimal and even if individual trees do torch, they present minimal radiant heating to the house.

Social/Economics

- The Fourmile Canyon Fire destroyed the highest (168) number of homes with the greatest loss in value ($220 million insured loss) in Colorado since 1976 when wildfire records started.
- Total fire management (suppression, emergency management, and post fire rehabilitation) was estimated at $14.1 million.
- County, State and Federal agencies partnered with landowners to treat approximately 600 acres within the area where Fourmile Canyon Fire burned.
- Projects administered by Colorado State Forest Service within and proximate to the fire perimeter totaled 823 acres at a total cost of $1,175,000 or $1,430 per acre.
- Boulder County Assessor's Office reports taxable property loss of $125 million resulting in a tax revenue loss in 2011 of $822,852 and a 2010 tax loss of $51,045.
- Interestingly, 127 of the landowners evacuated during the Fourmile Canyon Fire were surveyed in 2007 regarding their perceptions of their wildfire risk and mitigations efforts.
- Overall, survey respondents were fairly familiar with wildfire, with 83 percent reporting being somewhat or very aware of wildfire risk.
- Only 4 percent of the survey respondents reported not taking any actions to reduce their risks.
- A critical finding was that most landowners surveyed prior to the fire did not believe that characteristics of their home and immediate surroundings were significant factors influencing the likelihood of a wildfire damaging their property within the next 5 years.

Acknowledgments

The Fourmile Canyon Fire Assessment Team would like to offer the greatest thanks to individuals involved with or knowledgeable of the fire for their candor and responsiveness to our questions and requests for data, pictures, videos, and the myriad of other materials we collected. Compared to other fires we together and separately have reviewed, the quality and quantity of material to our disposal for this review was extraordinary. The Rocky Mountain Region, U.S. Forest Service, and the Colorado State Forest Service deserve special thanks for both the intellectual and financial support in making this project happen. As for all scientific endeavors, our work was greatly improved by the numerous and constructive comments we received from managers (Rocky Mountain Region, U.S. Forest Service, Colorado State Forest Service, U.S. Bureau of Land Management), stakeholders (25 county, State, and general public individuals) and the technical reviewers (Dr. Thomas Zimmerman, Dr. Elizabeth Reinhardt, Dr. Dave Peterson, Mr. Tim Sexton, Mr. Frankie Romero). All comments

USDA Forest Service Gen. Tech. Rep. RMRS-GTR-289. 2012

81

were reconciled and incorporated into the final product. Although such endeavors such as this review always seem to take longer than expected, the Team would like to thank the leadership of the Rocky Mountain Research Station for their support in the completion of the project. Most importantly we would like to thank Lane Eskew, Suzy Stephens, Nancy Chadwick, and Loa Collins of the publications staff, and Nan Christianson and Cass Cairns of the Communications Program for their usual high professionalism, talent, and work in making this publication possible.

References

Agee, J.K.; Skinner, C.N. 2005. Basic principles of forest fuel reduction treatments. Forest Ecology and Management. 211(1-2): 83-96.

Andrews, P.L.; Bevins, C.D.; Seli, R.C. 2008. BehavePlus fire modeling system, version 4.0: User's guide. Gen. Tech. Rep. RMRS-GTR-106WWW Revised. Fort Collins, CO: U.S. Department of Agriculture, Forest Service, Rocky Mountain Research Station. 116 p.

Boulder Incident Management Team (BIMT). 2010. After action review documents. Unpublished document on file at: Rocky Mountain Fire, Boulder, Colorado.

Brenkert-Smith, H.; Champ, P.A. 2011. Fourmile Canyon: Living with wildfire. Fire Management Today. 71(2): 33-39.

Butler, C.P. 1974. The urban/wildland fire interface. In: Proceedings of western states section/ Combustion Institute papers; 1974 May 6-7; Spokane, WA. Pullman, WA: Washington State University. 74(15): 1-17.

Calkin, David E.; Ager, Alan A.; Thompson, Matthew P., eds. 2011. A comparative risk assessment framework for wildland fire management: The 2010 cohesive strategy science report. Gen. Tech. Rep. RMRS-GTR-262. Fort Collins, CO: U.S. Department of Agriculture, Forest Service, Rocky Mountain Research Station. 63 p.

Carlson, J.D.; Bradshaw, Larry S.; Nelson, Ralph M., Jr.; [and others]. 2007. Application of the Nelson model to four timelag fuel classes using Oklahoma field observations: Model evaluation and comparison with national Fire Danger Rating System algorithms. International Journal of Wildland Fire. 16(2): 204-216.

Cohen, J.D. 1976. Analysis of Colorado mountain fire weather. In: Baker, D.H.; Fosberg, M.A., tech. coords. Proceedings of the fourth national conference on fire and forest meteorology; 1976 November 16–18; St. Louis, MO. Gen. Tech. Rep. RM-32. Fort Collins, CO: U.S. Department of Agriculture, Forest Service, Rocky Mountain Forest and Range Experiment Station: 38-41.

Cohen, J.D. 1995. Structure ignition assessment model (SIAM). In: Proceedings of the Biswell Symposium: Fire issues and solutions in urban interface and wildland ecosystems; 1994 February 15-17; Walnut Creek, CA. Gen. Tech. Rep. PSW-158. Albany, CA: U.S. Department of Agriculture, Forest Service, Pacific Southwest Research Station: 85-92.

Cohen, J.D. 2000a. A brief summary of my Los Alamos fire destruction examination. Wildfire. 9(4): 16-18.

Cohen, J.D. 2000b. Preventing disaster: Home ignitability in the wildland-urban interface. Journal of Forestry. 98(3): 15-21.

Cohen, J.D. 2008. The wildland-urban interface fire problem: A consequence of the fire exclusion paradigm. Forest History Today. Fall: 20-26.

Cohen, Jack D. 2004. Relating flame radiation to home ignition using modeling and experimental crown fires. Canadian Journal of Forest Research. 34(8): 1616-1626.

Cohen, J.D.; Butler, B.W. 1998. Modeling potential structure ignitions from flame radiation exposure with implications for wildland/urban interface fire management. In: Proceedings of the 13th fire and forest meteorology conference; 1996 October 27-31; Lorne, Australia. Moran, WY: International Association of Wildland Fire: 81-86.

Cohen, J.D.; Stratton, R.D. 2008. Home destruction examination: Grass Valley Fire. Tech. Pap. R5-TP-026b. Vallejo, CA: U.S. Department of Agriculture, Forest Service, Region 5. 26 p.

Cohen, Jack; Stratton, Rick D. 2003. Home destruction within the Hayman Fire perimeter. In: Graham, Russell T., tech. ed. Hayman Fire case study. Gen. Tech. Rep. RMRS-GTR-114. Ogden, UT: U.S. Department of Agriculture, Forest Service, Rocky Mountain Research Station: 263-292.

Cram, D.; Baker, T.; Boren, J. 2006. Wildland fire effects in silviculturally treated vs. untreated stands of New Mexico and Arizona. Res. Pap. RMRS-RP-55. Fort Collins, CO: U.S. Department of Agriculture, Forest Service, Rocky Mountain Research Station. 28 p.

Finney, M.A.; Bartlette, R.; Bradshaw L.; [and others]. 2003. Fire behavior, fuel treatments, and fire suppression on the Hayman Fire. In: Graham, Russell T., tech. ed. Hayman Fire case study. Gen. Tech. Rep. RMRS-GTR-114. Ogden, UT: U.S. Department of Agriculture, Forest Service, Rocky Mountain Research Station:. 33-180.

Finney, M.A.; McHugh, C.W.; Grenfell, I.C. 2005. Stand- and landscape-level effects of prescribed burning on two Arizona wildfires. Canadian Journal of Forest Research. 35(7): 1714-1722.

Foote, Ethan I.D. 1994. Structural survival on the 1990 Santa Barbara "Paint" fire: A retrospective study of urban-wildland interface fire hazard mitigation factors. University of California at Berkeley. Thesis,

Forthofer, J.M. 2007. Modeling wind in complex terrain for use in fire spread prediction. Fort Collins, CO: Colorado State University. Thesis. 123 p.

Gebert, K.M.; Calkin, D.E.; Yoder, J. 2007. Estimating suppression expenditures for individual large wildland fires. Western Journal of Applied Forestry. 22(3): 188-196.

Graham, R.T.; Jain, T.B.; Loseke, M. 2009. Fuel treatments, fire suppression, and their interaction with wildfire and its impacts: The Warm Lake experience during the Cascade Complex of wildfires in central Idaho, 2007. Gen. Tech. Rep. RMRS-GTR-229. Fort Collins, CO: U.S. Department of Agriculture, Forest Service, Rocky Mountain Research Station. 36 p.

Graham, R.T.; McCaffrey, S.; Jain, T.B., tech. eds. 2004. Science basis for changing forest structure to modify wildfire behavior and severity. Gen. Tech. Rep. RMRS-GTR-120. Fort Collins, CO: U.S. Department of Agriculture, Forest Service, Rocky Mountain Research Station. 43 p.

Graham, Russell T., tech. ed. 2003. Hayman Fire case study. Gen. Tech. Rep. RMRS-GTR-114. Ogden, UT: U.S. Department of Agriculture, Forest Service, Rocky Mountain Research Station. 396 p.

Graham, Russell T.; Harvey, Alan. E.; Jain, Theresa B.; Tonn, Jonalea R. 1999. The effects of thinning and similar stand treatments on fire behavior in western forests. Gen. Tech. Rep. PNW-GTR-463. Portland, OR: U.S. Department of Agriculture, Forest Service, Pacific Northwest Research Station. 27 p.

Howard, Ronald A.; North, D. Warner; Offensend, Fred L.; Smart, Charles N. 1973. Decision analysis of fire protection strategy for the Santa Monica Mountains: An initial assessment. Menlo Park, CA: Stanford Research Institute. 159 p.

Hudak, A. T.; Rickert, I.; Morgan, P.; [and others]. 2011. Review of fuel treatment effectiveness in forests and rangelands and a case study from the 2007 megafires in central Idaho USA. Gen. Tech. Rep. RMRS-GTR-252. Fort Collins, CO: U.S. Department of Agriculture, Forest Service, Rocky Mountain Research Station. 60 p.

Hunter, M.E.; Shepperd, W.D.; Lentile, J.E.; [and others]. 2007. A comprehensive guide to fuels treatment practices for ponderosa pine in the Black Hills, Colorado Front Range, and Southwest. Gen. Tech. Rep. RMRS-GTR-198. Fort Collins, CO: U.S. Department of Agriculture, Forest Service, Rocky Mountain Research Station. 93 p.

Jessen, Kenneth C. 2011. Colorado's best ghost towns. Loveland, CO: J. V. Publications. 136 p.

Keith, Robin P.; Veblen Thomas T.; Schoennagel, Tania L.; Sherriff, Rosemary L. 2010. Understory vegetation indicates historic fire regimes in ponderosa pine-dominated ecosystems in the Colorado Front Range. Journal of Vegetation Science. 21(3): 488-499.

Krasnow, K.; Schoennagel, T.; Veblen, T.T. 2009. Forest fuel mapping and evaluation of LAND-FIRE fuel maps in Boulder, County, Colorado, USA. Forest Ecology and Management 257(7): 1603-1612.

Kriederman, L. 2010. Fourmile Canyon Fire weather narrative. Fourmile Canyon Fire Incident Weather Meteorologist, National Weather Service, Boulder, CO.

LANDFIRE. 2010. LANDFIRE data overview. Washington, DC: U.S. Department of Agriculture, Forest Service; U.S. Department of the Interior. Online: http://www.landfire.gov/data_overviews.php. [June 15, 2012].

Loomis, J. 2004. Do nearby forest fires cause a reduction in residential property values? Journal of Forest Economics. 10(3): 149-157.

USDA Forest Service Gen. Tech. Rep. RMRS-GTR-289. 2012

83

Lynch, D.L.; Mackes, K. 2003. Costs for reducing fuels in Colorado forest restoration projects. In: Omi, P.N. ; Joyce, L.A., tech. eds. 2003. Fire, fuel treatments, and ecological restoration: Conference proceedings. Proceedings RMRS-P-29. Fort Collins, CO: U.S. Department of Agriculture, Forest Service, Rocky Mountain Research Station: 167-176

National Fire Protection Association (NFPA). 1989. The Black Tiger Fire case study. Quincy, MA: National Fire Protection Association, Fire Investigations Division. 40 p.

National Fire Protection Association (NFPA). 1992. Fire storm '91. Quincy, MA: National Fire Protection Association, Fire Investigations Division.. 30 p.

Nelson R.M., Jr. 2000. Prediction of diurnal change in 10-h fuel stick moisture content. Canadian Journal of Forest Research. 30(7): 1071-1087.

Pollet, J.; Omi, P.N. 2002. Effect of thinning and prescribed burning on crown fire severity in ponderosa pine forests. International Journal of Wildland Fire. 11(1): 1-10.

Prestemon, J.P.; Butry, D.T.; Abt, K.L.; Sutphen, R. 2010. Net benefits of wildfire prevention education efforts. Forest Science. 56(2): 181-192.

Rocky Mountain Area Coordinating Group (RMCG). 2009. Administrator talking points: Appropriate mobilization of resource aircraft. Issued July 2009. Unpublished document on file at: Rocky Mountain Area Coordination Center, Lakewood, CO.

Scott, Joe H.; Burgan, Robert E. 2005. Standard fire behavior fuel models: A comprehensive set for use with Rothermel's surface fire spread model. Gen. Tech. Rep. RMRS-GTR-153. Fort Collins, CO: U.S. Department of Agriculture, Forest Service, Rocky Mountain Research Station. 72 p.

Sherriff, R.L.; Veblen, T.T. 2007. A spatially-explicit reconstruction of historical fire occurrence in the ponderosa pine zone of the Colorado Front Range. Ecosystems. 10(2): 311-323.

Sherriff, R.L.; Veblen, T.T. 2008. Variability in fire-climate relationships in ponderosa pine forests in the Colorado Front Range. International Journal of Wildland Fire. 17(1): 50-59.

Stephens, Scott L.; Ruth, Lawrence W. 2005. Federal forest-fire policy in the United States. Ecological Applications. 15(2): 532-542.

Stettler, K.M.; Venn, T.J.; Calkin, D.E. 2010. The effects of wildfire and environmental amenities on property values in northwest Montana, USA. Ecological Economics. 69: 2233-2243.

Syphard, A.D.; Keeley, J.E.; Brennan, T.J. 2011. Factors affecting fuel break effectiveness in the control of large fires on the Los Padres National Forest, California. International Journal of Wildland Fire. 20(6): 764-775.

United States Department of Agriculture and Department of the Interior (USDA-DOI). 2011. Interagency standards for fire and aviation operations. NFES 2724. Boise, ID. National Interagency Fire Center.

United States Department of Agriculture and Natural Resources Conservation Service (USDA-NRCS). 2008. Soil survey of Boulder County area, Colorado. 288 p. http://soildatamart nrcs.usda.gov/manuscripts/CO643/0/Boulder%20CO643.pdf.

U.S. Government Accountability Office (GAO). 2009. Additional documentation of agency experiences with good neighbor authority could enhance its future. GAO-09-277. Washington, DC: U.S. Government Accountability Office. 53 p.

Veblen, T.T.; Kitzberger, T.; Donnegan, J. 2000. Climatic and human influences on fire regimes in ponderosa pine forests in the Colorado Front Range. Ecological Applications. 10(4): 1178-1195.

Weaver, H. 1943. Fire as an ecological and silvicultural factor in the ponderosa pine region of the Pacific slope. Journal of Forestry. 41(1): 7-14.

Appendix A: Senator Udall's Letter _____

MARK UDALL
COLORADO

SUITE SH-317
SENATE HART OFFICE BUILDING
WASHINGTON, DC 20510
(202) 224-5941

United States Senate

WASHINGTON, DC 20510

September 15, 2010

The Honorable Bill Ritter, Jr.
Governor
State of Colorado
136 State Capitol
Denver, CO 80203

The Honorable Tom Vilsack
Secretary
U.S. Department of Agriculture
1400 Independence Ave., S.W.
Washington, DC 20250

Dear Governor Ritter and Secretary Vilsack:

I had the opportunity to tour the Fourmile Canyon Fire area after it was effectively contained on Monday, September 13. I was struck by the severity of this fire and the substantial loss of property. This tour was a humbling reminder of the heroic efforts conducted by first responders in attacking the fire and making sure that people were evacuated to safety, resulting, thankfully, with no lives being lost.

I was also struck by the seemingly indiscriminate nature of the burn areas and how some houses and structures were spared while others—in some cases right next door—were totally destroyed. Like the destructive Hayman Fire in 2002, I think the experience of this fire may provide some lessons on the nature of wildfires along the Front Range and can help provide some useful information on how we might better respond to and mitigate such damage when future fires occur.

Shortly after the Hayman Fire, I asked the U.S. Forest Service to conduct a study to review the fire and its behavior so that we could learn from that experience. The result was a useful report that examined this fire from many angles. I am writing today to seek a similar study of the Fourmile Canyon Fire. Since this fire included many non-federal as well as some federal lands, I am suggesting that this review be jointly convened by the state and the U.S. Forest Service.

As you know, the Fourmile Canyon Fire in Colorado occurred in an area where previous wildfires had occurred and where some small, fuels-reduction projects were conducted. This area includes both wildland-urban interface zones and areas of high natural resource values, including wildlife habitats and important watersheds. I believe it would be instructive to take a close look at the behavior of this fire, examine the factors that led to its intensity, and see if the way it behaved when it encountered these previously affected or treated areas can be instructive in designing future risk-reduction projects.

I also believe we should examine the use of the aerial firefighting resources (tankers and helicopters), because questions have been raised about the availability, quality and costs of these resources in attacking this fire.

In addition, once the immediate crisis is over, it will be necessary to start making decisions about ways to begin restoration of this and other burned areas. In this instance, too, the Fourmile Canyon Fire area could be a very useful case study to determine what can and should be done after such a large fire to prevent or minimize erosion and other damage. Sound, cost-effective restoration methods will be especially important in light of the severe drain on the Forest Service's funds caused by the need to fight so many large fires, which will make it that much harder to finance critical restoration work.

Accordingly, I suggest that the U.S. Forest Service and the Colorado State Forest Service establish a "Fourmile Canyon Fire Review Panel" composed of local, state and federal experts to explore these issues and help guide future decisions. Its purpose would be to focus on the future, rather than attempt to assign blame for past events, and as a balanced panel including experts with varied backgrounds, it might well have wider credibility with various groups than would a panel of less broad membership.

As soon as practicable—and after all the needs related to managing the Fourmile Canyon Fire and the Reservoir Road Fire have been completed—I suggest that this review get started on looking at the following issues (this is not meant to be an exhaustive or exclusive list of topics):

1.   What conditions – including fuel, forest structure, prior fuel treatment, topography, weather, wind and land ownership – affected the behavior and intensity of the fire? To what degree did these factors influence where the fire was stopped, how hot the fire burned, whether soil was damaged, etc.?

2.   What was the effectiveness of thinning treatments on lands in the area in stopping or slowing the fire, reducing fire intensity, and reducing soil damage?

3.   What was the effectiveness of prescribed burns in influencing the fire?

4.   To what extent did the fire behave differently (all other factors being equal) in roaded and unroaded areas?

5.   To what degree and under what circumstances were firefighting activities successful/not successful in limiting the spread of the fire (e.g. bulldozing firelines)? Were the aerial suppression resources timely, readily available and effective in attacking the fire (when those resources could be applied safely)? To what extent was controlling the fire dependent on the weather? How effectively was money/resources spent in fighting the fire?

6.   What factors influenced which structures burned?

7.   To what extent were local or county regulations followed with respect to defensible space or other fire-related policies? To what extent does variation in these policies account for structures saved or lost?

8. What science exists to determine the effectiveness of varying post-fire restoration treatments?

9. What types of transparent monitoring protocol and reports (for forest regrowth, water monitoring, sedimentation, endangered species recovery, etc.) should the various jurisdictions put in place to continue to learn from the fire?

10. Under what circumstances and across what areas can/should control areas be established to observe natural recovery?

As you know, it is imperative to put a high priority on reducing the risk of catastrophic fires to communities in the wildland-urban interface as we work to restore the natural, beneficial role of fire in forest ecosystems. I think a review panel along the lines suggested above will help to build greater consensus about how to move toward those goals.

And, even though the bark beetle epidemic and other insect infestations may not have had an effect on this fire, this review and the lessons learned from this fire also may have value and application in areas heavily impacted by insects and disease.

I look forward to working with both of you on this important review.

Sincerely,

Mark E. Udall
U.S. Senator

USDA Forest Service Gen. Tech. Rep. RMRS-GTR-289. 2012

87

Appendix B: Response to Manager Comments Received on Preliminary Draft _____

U.S. Forest Service, Rocky Mountain Region (Region-2)

Overall Assessment Comments

- A list of individuals contacted to provide input to the report needs to be included. Without such a list, it is not possible to determine the basis for some statements in the report. For example, on page 34 a statement is made that the review team did not find documentation that described intended treatment performance. Without a list of contacted individuals it is not possible to determine if this information does not exist or if the team did not contact individuals that could be expected to have that information.

  Response: Names will not be provided as to protect the individuals contacted and not jeopardize such future interactions that will likely be desired and/or required in future fire reviews. However, the numbers of individuals contacted and their respective agency affiliations are included.

- There is too much focus in the report on the lack of treatment of surface fuels with prescribed fire after mechanical hazardous fuels reduction treatments, and how the lack of such treatments led to higher fire intensities. Most local fire managers will agree with this assessment; however, the team misses critical information regarding why this situation exists. There are several substantial barriers to implementing prescribed fire in this area:
  - Landownership: A majority of the lands that were treated were private; private land ownership patterns and potential liability make use of prescribed fire problematic on these lands.
  - Public perceptions of fire risk: The public in general likely does not support use of prescribed fire due to potential risk of escape.
  - Public health: Based on past experience, there are likely a number of persons living in this area that could be adversely affected by smoke.
  - Regulation of prescribed fire smoke: Current regulations create severe limits on any widespread use of prescribed fire in this area.

  Response: Fuel treatment effectiveness was specifically identified by Senator Udall in his request for the review. Further, the efficacy of treatments in changing fire spread and intensity emerged as one of the most relevant and interesting topics found in this review. Our intention was to conduct a scientific review of the physical event, specifically the interaction of the Fourmile Fire and the treatments within the fire perimeter and not describe the social context and ownership constraints under which these treatments were developed.

- Please provide additional supporting references to the document rather than vague "body of knowledge" statements currently utilized.

Response: *We provide a minimal set of relevant citations. The purpose of this review was not to provide a comprehensive review of fuel treatments or their efficacy with the occurrence of wildfire. The review is specific to the Fourmile Canyon Fire and those interested in the current state of scientific knowledge are directed towards the relevant research cited and the abundant references in them.*

- Throughout the report, a heavy emphasis is placed on aerial retardant use and conjecture on its effectiveness (text, figures, many photos and maps). Tanker gallons are a nice, quantifiable statistic. Little mention is made of strategic placement of fire control features by fire managers. This retardant bias probably misrepresents actual effectiveness. Retardant was used effectively by the Type 3 organization and the IMTs, but drop locations are often coincidental with fire perimeter once extreme fire behavior has passed. Fire spread and behavior subsided primarily due to moderated weather conditions, which coincided with increased use of aviation resources.

Response*: We agree with this statement. We can only report the limited factual information available after the event. Again the Senator's letter specifically asked the review to address the availability and use of air tankers. We agree with the statement regarding the coincidence of moderated weather and suppression effectiveness.*

- The maps on page 35 are too small to be useful to the reader.

Response: *The figure was redrafted and made into three separate figures.*

- The location of the pictures in the report should be identified.

Response*: Corrected where appropriate. However, specific house locations were not identified.*

Introduction

- Page 3: May be a technical detail, but fire spread conditions of Fourmile were not "very similar to those experienced by the Black Tiger fire in 1989 and the Hayman in 2002." Those fires were both summer-time events; Black Tiger was an extremely hot day, the fire was driven by up-slope winds; Fourmile was a down slope, "Chinook" wind-driven event with extremely low humidity and mild temperatures.

Response: *From a technical fire behavior standpoint, the seasonal timing and characteristics of the synoptic event were not important. To illustrate the irrelevancy of season, the Fourmile Canyon Fire was a summer time event, while Hayman occurred in spring. Regardless, the primary fire behavior characteristics were in fact very similar among these fires. These issues were highlighted in the text.*

- On page 3 a reference is made to "prized" recreation lands. While some of the areas burned are important for recreation, to suggest they are more important or "prized" than many similar lands along the Front Range is inaccurate.

Response: *Removed*

USDA Forest Service Gen. Tech. Rep. RMRS-GTR-289. 2012

89

Methods

- Page 6; Methods: Data collection lists U.S. Forest Service, but they did not talk to me and to my knowledge, did not interview the District FMO of the ARF South Zone, which surrounds the Fourmile fire area. Nor did the researchers interview the ARF fire line supervisors involved in initial attack, the ARF overhead assigned to extended attack, the dispatchers in the FTC Interagency Fire Center, or show evidence of any photos from the ARF. They did collect some info from the air tanker base manager, which would only provide a very limited view of a support function, not intimate fire knowledge.

  Response: The science team made a strong effort to interview relevant individuals involved in the fire, especially the local fire districts and volunteer fireman who were initial responders. Given the complexity of the fire and the number of jurisdictions, individuals may have been overlooked but we feel that the omissions that may have occurred do not take away from the findings that we present. In reconciling the comments, efforts were made to gather additional relevant opinions where warranted.

Physical Setting

- On page 13 there is a reference to "endemic levels" of mountain pine beetle (mpb) activity. While I agree that mpb activity likely was not a major factor in this fire, I'm not sure that the reference to endemic levels of activity is accurate either. The references cited would not have the most up-to-date data related to mpb activity in this area. Were USDA, Forest Service or Colorado State Forest Service forest health personnel contacted regarding current levels of mpb activity? Were the latest mpb progression maps reviewed?

  Response: Yes, we reviewed pertinent Aerial Detection Survey Data (ADS) available for Region-2, Forest Service and the report has been modified to clarify the data reviewed in the Physical Setting Discussion.

Pre-Fire Fuel Treatments

- We would encourage the review team to explicitly state that the findings regarding fuels treatment effectiveness on the Fourmile Canyon Fire may or may not be transferable to other locations.

  Response: The review team is very familiar with the research regarding fuel treatment effectiveness over the range of ponderosa pine forests as indicated by the citations provided, and many of these findings are transferrable to similar vegetative communities. Statements to this effect are included.

- We request that you include statements that refer to the demonstrated effectiveness of fuels treatments in other wildfire situations, including the recent Wallow fire in Arizona, and provide references to the growing body of literature on fuel treatment effectiveness. The performance of fuel treatments in wildfire situations has been documented in multiple evaluations including Jimerson and Jones 2000, USDA 2007, USDA 2007a, USDA 2008, and Graham and others 2009. Key findings from these references include:

  - Where fuels had been treated, fire behavior was noticeably different from that which occurred in neighboring untreated fuels. Most fuel treatments reduced fire behavior from a crown fire to a surface fire.

- Treatment location and juxtaposition and the treatments of surface fuels, ladder fuels, and crown fuels (in order of importance) are major determinates of both wildfire intensity and burn severity.

- The presence of fuels treatments directly impacted the survivability of structures. Area fuel treatments adjacent to subdivisions provided important safety zones, increasing suppression effectiveness, which saved houses. Fuel treatments, when of sufficient size, often provide safe zones for firefighters.

- Fuel treatments influence burn severity. A higher proportion of acres burned severely on untreated lands than where fuel or other vegetation treatments had been applied. Reduced fire severity in fuels treatments that result in remnant trees and green vegetation will lead to more rapid vegetative recovery compared to high severity areas where all trees are black. Fuel treatments that create irregular forest structures and compositions, both within and among stands (macro and micro mosaics), tend to produce wildfire resilient forests.

- Some fuel treatment units burned at high fire intensity because they were adjacent and downwind from untreated units. Crown fire momentum carried high fire intensity partway into these treated areas before the more widely spaced crowns and reduced surface fuel caused the fire to fall to the surface.

- Fuel treatment longevity and effectiveness are dependent on location, dead and live fuel ratios, and rate, composition, and structure of vegetation recovery. More recent fuel treatments and higher intensity fuel treatments reduced fire behavior and fire effects more effectively than older and less intense treatments. Incomplete or partial treatments are less effective or can be ineffective. Large fuel removal alone, without the follow-up treatment of smaller diameter fuels, may not provide adequate fuels reduction to prevent a fire from becoming stand-replacing.

- Fuel treatments increase suppression effectiveness. By modifying the fire's behavior, fuel treatments present suppression opportunities that otherwise may not have been available. When Incident Management Teams had knowledge of treatments, they used these treated areas to plan and implement suppression. These opportunities include both providing locations for burnouts to placement of hand and machine fire lines. Decreased fire intensity in fuel treatments allow fire crews to more easily suppress spot fires that may ignite.

- Even in the face of extreme fire behavior, treated areas may slow the spread of the fire and disrupt the fire's progress.

- Treating only a portion of the understory may be ineffective as crown fire momentum from adjacent untreated areas will carry high fire intensity in the overstory and may continue as crown fire in the treated stand.

- The longevity of the fuel treatment depends on the type of treatment and the vegetation type. The period of effectiveness may be a relatively short time for fuels with a simple structure such as grasslands, or many years in more complex fuel types such as multi-storied coniferous forests.

Response: *The science team is very knowledgeable regarding the scientific litera-ture on fuel treatment effects. We did not consider internal reports identified as appropriate literature for inclusion in this review. We provided the most relevant citations within the scientific literature. The purpose of this review was not to provide a comprehensive review of fuel treatment effects. Those interested in the current state of scientific knowledge are directed towards the relevant research included within the document and the numerous citations within the cited docu-ments (Weaver 1943, Pollet and Omi 2002, Graham and others 2004, Agee and Skinner 2005, Finney and others 2005, Cram and others 2006, Hunter and others 2007, Graham and others 2009, Hudak and others 2011).*

- The period of time over which fuel treatments remain effective depends on:
  - The type and intensity of the treatment;
  - The number of fuel layers involved;
  - The rate of accumulation of fuels; and
  - Fuel decomposition rates, and other factors.

Between 2006 and 2011, about 600 assessments were completed by the Forest Service and the Bureau of Land Management on wildfires that burned into areas where hazardous fuels reduction treatments had previously been conducted. These assessments evaluated the effects of prescribed fire and mechanical and chemical treatments on fire behavior and fire suppression actions. The data indicate that such treatments helped to alter wildfire activity and control wildfires about 90 percent of the time (USDA Forest Service 2011). In most of these cases for which data are available, treatments such as thinning, mowing, and prescribed burning aided firefighters in controlling the fires; furthermore, fires changed from active crown fires (burning an entire upper story of the forest) to passive crown fires (where only a single tree or small group of trees burned), or from passive crown fires to surface fires.

Response: *The science team is aware of the scientific literature on fuel treatment effects and efficacy in response to wildfire. We did not consider internal reports identified as appropriate literature for inclusion in this review. We provided the most relevant citations within the scientific literature. The purpose of this review was not to provide a comprehensive review of fuel treatment effects. Those interested in the current state of scientific knowledge are directed towards the relevant research included within the document and the citations included in them. Moreover, the 90 percent statistic provided is not relevant to the discussion of the effectiveness of fuel treatments as it is derived from self-reporting within fuel treatment database.*

- Clarify intent of fuels treatments by providing additional detail in the report nar-rative such as:
  - All fuel treatments are performed to modify burning conditions. The fuel treatments are not performed to prevent fires but to alter fuel profiles so that public and firefighter safety is improved and communities, watershed, infrastructure, and other values-at-risk are less vulnerable to impacts from wildfire. The goals of the treatments are to achieve some combination of (a) reducing flammability, (b) reducing fire intensity, (c) reducing the potential for creating firebrands (spotting) and crown fires, and (d) increasing firefighter safety and effectiveness.

    ○ The amount of land to be treated around communities and other values-at-risk, to reduce the threat depends on the current structure of the vegetation, fuel loadings, topographic location, fire regime type, and firefighting concerns such as access.

    ○ The ease of control of wildland fire is directly related to fire behavior, which is a primary consideration for public and firefighter safety. Although some factors contributing to fire behavior are unchangeable (i.e., weather, topography, and vegetation), factors that can be changed to ease the difficulty of controlling a wildland fire are keeping fires on the ground rather than crown fires, and opening up the canopy to allow water and retardant to reach the ground fuels as well as to provide for ease of fire-line construction.

    ○ Fuel treatments alter fire behavior characteristics that influence crown fire initiation and spread. Furthermore, even if thinning didn't directly contribute to moderating fire behavior, it could indirectly contribute by providing better access and removing obstacles for safe and effective fire control and by providing a strategic base for fire-line construction.

__Response:__ We described available information, as contained in the project statements of work, on the stated intent of treatments that occurred in the area where the Fourmile Canyon Fire burned. We have made modification to the text to expand discussion of treatment intention. In general, we argue that mitigation efforts such as mechanical fuel treatments should be designed to reduce expected loss under those conditions where loss is likely to occur. In general, we could not find evidence that treatments were effective in reducing expected loss and, therefore, did not achieve objectives, stated or otherwise.

• As currently worded, the document includes "Firewise" treatments and stand level treatments all in the category of fuels treatments. We believe it is important that the report distinguish between "Firewise" treatments conducted around homes and stand level treatments as the implications for maintenance are extremely different. Homeowners can maintain annual grass and shrub production on a regular basis where stand level treatments will not be operationally mowed or burned on an annual basis.

__Response:__ We do not use the term "Firewise" within the document. We distinguish between wildland fuel treatments and activities that occurred within the Home Ignition Zone (HIZ). Differentiation between funded activities within or proximate to the HIZ was not possible with the available spatial data.

• Please consider adding a statement to the discussion of fuels treatment prescriptions related to the social license necessary to achieve implementation on private lands. In the interface it often requires a negotiation process and some effectiveness may be traded away in order to make inroads into implementing any treatments at all.

__Response:__ The focus of this review was to evaluate discernible physical effects of treatments that occurred. We did not consider the social and political environment under which treatments were designed and implemented.

• Provide additional detail showing the acreage for treatments by the treatment types and display those types on Figure 15.

Response: We assume the comment is in reference to Figure 21. For many of the treatments, we were not able to spatially distinguish treated area by type. Additionally, from our analysis the efficacy of fuel treatments in either modifying fire behavior or burn severity did not vary based on treatment type; therefore, we did not feel that distinguishing among types was relevant nor would change the discussion on fuel treatment efficacy during the Fourmile Canyon Fire.

- Please clarify the statements regarding Photo 8 that would indicate that the treatment displayed in the photos was not effective when all visual evidence indicates that the treatments were highly effective.

Response: Within this draft, the geographic juxtaposition in Figure 24 does not validate treatment effect without understanding localized burning conditions and fire exposure.

- Please clarify caption for Photo 12. The bottom photo labeled "surface backing fire" shows evidence of individual and group torching, which is not the same as surface fire.

Response: This is Figure 33 within the draft. We agree that there is some evidence of tree torching; however, we still consider this as a representation of a "surface backing fire."

- Please clarify what definition of effectiveness the review team utilized to determine whether the treatments were effective on the Fourmile Canyon Fire. Since the CSFS did not fully define the design criteria for the treatments it is difficult to understand what standard the review team is utilizing to determine whether the treatments were effective or not.

Response: From the broadest perspective, effectiveness can be defined in terms of reduced loss. As the report states, the broad objectives were to change fire behavior to (1) decrease burn severity, (2) change the fire's rate of spread, and (3) facilitate suppression activities. We were unable to identify evidence of these objectives being met by the fuel treatments when the Fourmile Canyon Fire burned. An additional identified objective was to improve the safety of roads. We were unable to determine if and when individuals utilized the roads during the fire where treatments occurred and, more importantly, if the treatments made a difference in how the roads were or were not used. Moreover, we were unable to ascertain when or how these areas burned, or would have burned, in the absence of treatment. We agree that clearly designed criteria for measuring treatment effectiveness is critical for demonstrating the value of fuels management activities.

- Please clarify the role that wind sheltering played in the north slopes' not experiencing much fire. It appears that the findings indicate that the primary reason the north slopes did not burn was because they were Douglas-fir. Please explain the role sheltering played and the difference in burning if the wind had aligned with the drainages.

Response: North facing slopes had a variety of characteristics that could not be isolated as to their relationship with fire behavior or burn severity: (1) winds, (2) vegetative community, (3) fuels composition and structure, and (4) micro-climate (e.g. fuel moisture) associated with north facing slopes. In addition, our analysis of winds showed that the winds on both the north and south facing slopes were very erratic and the winds did not necessarily align with topography. Therefore, distinguishing the effects of vegetation composition (e.g., Douglas-fir) or wind sheltering was not feasible.

Fire Suppression

- September 6th bullet: Please incorporate the following talking points related to aircraft use from the previously provided RMCG Briefing papers.

  o Winds in excess of 25 to 30 miles per hour make aircraft dropping suppressants and retardant ineffective due to drift created by the strong winds. Strong winds can increase risks to aircraft and flight crews. Depending on wind speed, topography and fire conditions, there can be moderate to severe turbulence at lower "drop" altitudes.

  o Aerial (retardant or suppression) resources are utilized in conjunction with ground fire fighters for maximum suppression results. Fire fighters put the fires out, not aircraft.

  Response: *Text was modified to include discussion of conditions on why aviation was not utilized prior to the evening of September 6. In addition, information suggests that the extensive use of retardant on September 7 occurred with limited ground suppression resource support.*

Fuel Treatment Efficacy

- Please add additional detail to this section that enumerates whether the treatments burned with Low, Moderate or High Severity.

  Response: *Adequately discussed in response to previous comments.*

- Third Bullet: Please provide clarification on the difference between annual maintenance in "Firewise" treatments and stand level treatments. The first, which is a homeowner's responsibility, can be done more readily than operationally in stand level treatments.

  Response: *Adequately discussed in response to previous comments.*

- Fourth Bullet: Figure 20, What is the imagery date, source, and resolution for the infrared photography? Please clarify the term "vegetative burn severity" as it is not a commonly used severity term. What element of vegetation is the severity of burned/black referring to?

  Response: *This is Figure 43. WorldView satellite Imagery is from Digital Globe and displayed as false color (infrared) and was taken on September 12, 2010 at 1159 hours. Cell resolution is 6 feet (2 meters). This same satellite imagery is used in figures 44 and 47 for the fuel treatments, and changes were made to the figures.*

- We would suggest using the Burned Area Reflectance Classification (BARC) Imagery that is available for the Fourmile Canyon Fire as it is easier to see differences in severity than with the imagery currently used. BARC maps display four category severity classification subset values:

USDA Forest Service Gen. Tech. Rep. RMRS-GTR-289. 2012

95

0 = background/fill
1 = unchanged / very low (Dark Green)
2 = low severity (Cyan)
3 = moderate severity (Yellow)
4 = high severity (Red)
Instead of just burned/black or unburned.

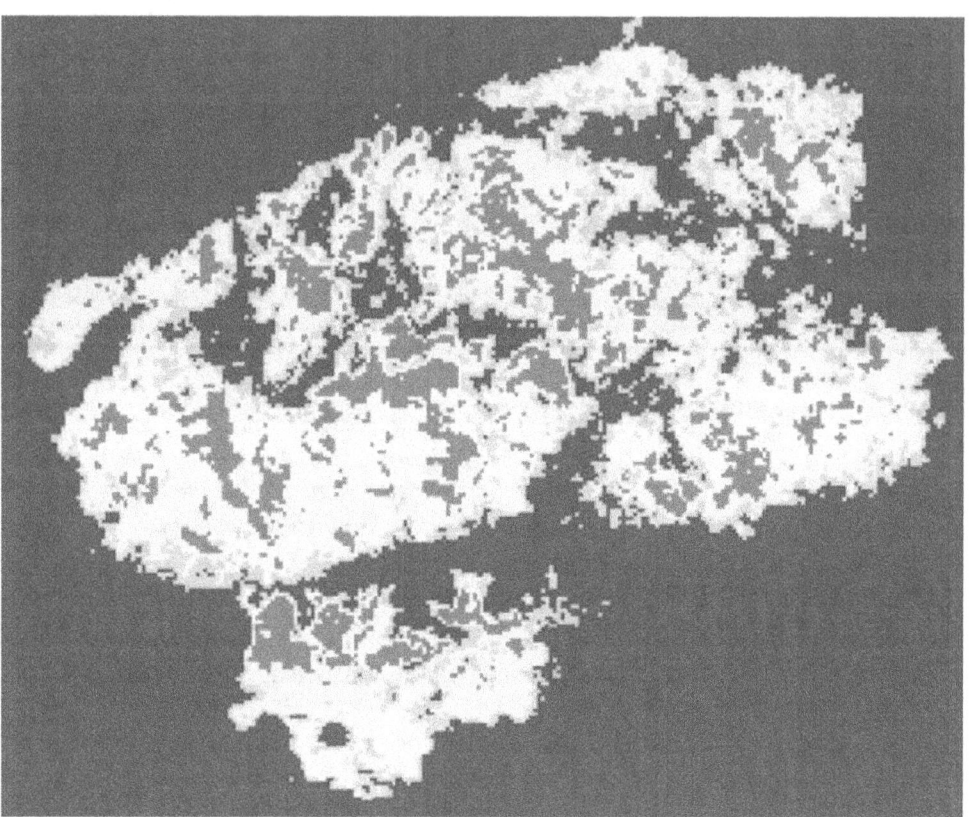

- The BARC Imagery appears to indicate moderate severity over much of the fire area and it is more descriptive of the fire area than "vegetative" severity, which appears to differentiate only on the basis of "burned or black" and "unburned."

- Visually overlaying the fuels treatments over the BARC imagery appears to provide a different view than treatments burned more intensely than non-treatments. In fact some, especially in the southern portion of the fire, indicate low severity in treated areas compared to non-treated areas.

Response: BARC imagery is a product developed for the purposes of watershed rehabilitation efforts following wildfire events. Categories of "burn severity" distinguished by BARC maps are based on national standards and do not apply equally across vegetation types or between forest and non-forest communities. The basis of BARC classification is in change in infrared reflectance caused by green vegetation being burned; grasslands or open forests (particularly after curing of grasses) are often biased towards classification of moderate or low severity due to vegetation being less altered than burned forest (see Safford and others 2008 (Ecosystems 11: 1-11), Miller and Thode 2007 (Remote Sensing of Environment

109: 66-80), and Miller and others 2009 (Remote Sensing of the Environment 113: 645-656). In addition, BARC maps can be reclassified (e.g., thresholds changed) to reflect the desires of the user. As illustrated in the Web site http://www.fs.fed. us/eng/rsac/baer/barc.html, "For example, if you believe not enough "unburned" pixels are represented in the image, in the "Symbol" field, click on a few of the "low" colored boxes and change the color to dark green. Observe how the BARC patterns change as you change the thresholds. After looking at your ancillary data and deciding more changes need to be made, continue with the same process as described above." The imagery we used does not rely on classification rules and presents the most accurate and precise (2 meter resolution versus 20 to 30 meter for BARC) representation available as to how vegetation was burned or not burned.

- Please clarify that in the case of Photo 23 and the unburned piles, that since they were not burned it was not a completed treatment and should not be determined to be effective or ineffective based on an incompleted treatment stream.

Response: This is Figure 45 in the current draft. A revised figure and expanded description is included.

- Figure 22: Please use BARC imagery to determine severity. Simply saying that an area is burned or black is not an indication of effectiveness. Fuel treatments are meant to burn and simply comparing whether they burned or did not burn is a meaningless comparison.

Response: See comment above.

- Fourth Bullet: Please clarify what is meant by "in some cases" treatments burned more severely than untreated areas. Was that <10%? >50%?

Response: Visual evidence clearly suggests this outcome; however, quantification of these levels is beyond the scope of this study.

- Page 15, 1st Bullet: Please clarify the difference between why the green trees around the home in photo 17 are an effective treatment but the green trees in photo 8 are not effective as indicated in the narrative starting on page 5. Also please clarify that in the case of photo 17 the treatment of the surface fuels was actually the landowner mowing and weed whacking annual grass production as part of landscape and Firewise maintenance.

Response: These are Figures 46 and 24 in current draft respectively. We have specific information regarding surface and canopy fuel mitigation efforts demonstrated within Figure 46. We do not specifically discuss treatment effectiveness in either figure.

- Page 15, 2nd Bullet: Please clarify this statement. Did the relationship make it difficult to identify issues with effectiveness or ???

Response: We provide additional information within the current draft.

- Figure 24: Please also show the relationship to burn severity using BARC.

Response: See previous comments regarding BARC imagery.

USDA Forest Service Gen. Tech. Rep. RMRS-GTR-289. 2012

97

- While dwelling on the lack of prescribed fire and the effects of such on fire intensity, there is little or no discussion in the report related to whether projected benefits of fuels reduction treatments were achieved. On page 34, the potential benefits anticipated from the hazardous fuels treatments are listed. The first benefit is "create road corridors that allow safe travel for homeowners leaving and firefighters entering a wildfire area." Given the safe evacuation of the area, it would appear this benefit was achieved, but this is not mentioned as a finding. The second fire related benefit is to "create a wildfire defendable zone using shaded fire break … near homes and communities." While defensible space is discussed, the benefits of fuels treatments in reducing risk to homes and communities is not adequately addressed. A quick review of maps on pages 18 and 29 indicates that there are probably 4 to 6 areas where adjacent fuels treatments may have reduced risk to adjacent homes or communities during the fire. So, it appears likely that the two primary benefits anticipated from fuels treatments were achieved yet the review team fails to identify this as a finding.

  Response: Please see previous response regarding the absence of reduced burn severity in treated areas. We were unable to determine if treated corridors were used during fire impingement of these areas and we do not have the ability to develop counterfactual simulation of the conditions under which the fire would have burned had the treatments not been conducted.

- In two places, on pages 47 and 51, it is pointed out that fuels treatments were utilized in conjunction with retardant drops to limit fire expansion. However, this finding of success was not carried through the report to the findings summary.

  Response: Comments were on an earlier draft. New evidence suggests that treatment, retardant drop, and fire spread did not coincide within the area around Bald Mountain. We have updated the current draft accordingly.

- The review team focuses almost exclusively on failings of fuels treatments on the first day of the fire. Given burning conditions that day, some level of failure of fuels treatments was likely. The review team does not discuss benefits of fuels treatments on subsequent days of the fire in limiting additional fire expansion and providing areas where the fire could be attacked successfully. There is little discussion of possible reasons why the fire did not again expand on September 9th through the 11th. On page 63 there is a statement that "they (fuels treatments) were probably of limited value to fire containment efforts on September 6th." It has been reported that fuels treatments in conjunction with retardant drops were beneficial to preventing the fire from moving into the community of Gold Hill late on the 6th.

  Response: Research evidence from other fires under extreme fire conditions suggests that fire behavior did respond to fuel treatments that included prescribed fire. During this fire we were unable to determine fuel treatment effect on the first day. Fire weather moderated in subsequent days so there was little engagement between fire spread and treated areas. Again we argue that treatments should be designed to reduce loss under conditions where loss is most likely to occur.

Home Destruction

- Please provide reference to Finney and Cohen 2003 and distinguish the difference between treatments (both purpose and intensity) in the wildlands (landscape scale) and the Home Ignition Zone (local scale). For hazardous fuels management to create the desired effect on fire behavior, management strategies must address the local and landscape scales. Local scale addresses effects of fire within a forest stand, treatment unit, or adjacent to or including the area around a house or other structure (Finney and Cohen 2003).

    Response: We agree that clearly identifying the strategic objectives of treatment programs is critical to success. Reference to Finney and Cohen (2003) has been expanded.

- Page 69-71: The report makes a direct correlation between numbers of engines/water tenders available, to the number of homes destroyed. This seems over-simplified, since the event is a dynamic, advancing wildland fire, not a single point-source (structure) fire in which fixed attack by engines is effective. It seems unfounded to imply that increased numbers of engines would have decreased home destruction.

    Response: The intent of the discussion was not to imply effectiveness of the engines but to emphasize how fire conditions and residential exposure to fire brands and flames exceeded any reasonable level of protection.

- The findings on the "Home Ignition Zone" are quantifiable and the emphasis on the success of pre-ignition efforts by homeowners is well documented. Hopefully this message/finding is well publicized.

    Response: Agreed. No further clarification or edits were made.

- On page 78 I believe there is a typographical error in the last sentence of the 2nd paragraph.

    Response: Fixed.

Social/Economic

Fire Management Costs

- 4th Suppression Bullet: Please clarify the significance of the SCI being more than 1 standard deviation than the SCI and how that relates to the percentile classes in the SCI displayed in WFDSS.

    Response: Discussion has been changed to focus on percentile classes for improved clarity.

- Please explain why this SCI does not agree with the SCI that was prepared for the WFDSS decision and is part of the published WFDSS decision. If the average suppression cost was $1634/acre it was less than the 90th percentile, which for a WUI fire seems to be a lower cost than usually exhibited for WUI fires.

USDA Forest Service Gen. Tech. Rep. RMRS-GTR-289. 2012

99

Response: The SCI within WFDSS was based on projected fire size of 7500 acres not the actual fire size of 6181. Fire size is an important variable in predicting average fire costs within the SCI model. There is no clear and consistent definition of WUI fire that we know of. Reference is made of how the Fourmile Canyon Fire had a high level of residential exposure relative to most fires. However, we do not have models that suggest average fire costs for these types of wildfires that present extensive private residential loss.

- Page 86, of interest only to ARF Line Officers and fire personnel: Of the 37 "significant" fires in Colorado since 1976, 9 have been in the FTC Zone.

Response: Correction noted.

Summary

- On page 89, a statement is made related to slash piles burning in a treatment unit adjacent to Gold Hill. While the statement is correct, there should also be a discussion regarding the homes adjacent to the unit, which was a primary reason for placement of the treatment unit.
- Also on page 89 is a statement that placement of units adjacent to roads and ridges confounds treatment effects. It is unclear what is confounded. Strategic placement of fuels treatments to take advantage of topographic or vegetation changes is smart management. If the roads were successfully used as evacuation routes and if homes survived then the treatments were successful.
- We would encourage the review team to explicitly state that the findings regarding fuels treatment effectiveness on the Fourmile Canyon Fire may or may not be transferable to other locations.
- Please enumerate how the treatments burned by BARC severity Classes.
- Page 23, 1st bullet: If the treatments focused on forest health, were they truly fuels treatments?
- Page 23 4th bullet: Please provide distinction between stand level and Firewise treatments as it relates to maintenance of grass and herbaceous fuel loads.
- Page 23 5th bullet: Please clarify what is meant by a "in some cases" treatments burned more severely than untreated areas. Was that <10%? >50%? As suggested above we believe a more valuable comparison would be to utilize the BARC severity classes rather than simple interpretations of burned or unburned using infrared imagery.

Response: The summary has been changed where appropriate to reflect the changes made in the body of the paper.

References

Finney, Mark A.; Cohen, Jack D. 2003. Expectation and evaluation of fuel management objectives. Proceedings RMRS-P-29. U.S. Department of Agriculture, Forest Service, Rocky Mountain Research Station. 475 p.

Graham, Russell T.; Jain, Theresa B.; Loseke, Mark. 2009. Fuel treatments, fire suppression, and their interaction with wildfire and its impacts: The Warm Lake experience during the Cascade Complex of wildfires in central Idaho, 2007. Gen. Tech.Rep. RMRS-GTR-229. Fort Collins, CO: U.S. Department of Agriculture, Forest Service, Rocky Mountain Research Station. 36 p.

Jimerson, Thomas M.; Jones, David W. 2000. Ecological and watershed implications of the Megram Fire. In: Fire Conference 2000: The First Congress on fire ecology, prevention and management; Nov. 27–Dec. 1, 2000; San Diego, CA. http://www.humboldt.edu/extended/klamath/proceedings2001/KLAMSYM6.PDF [July 3, 2012].

U.S. Department of Agriculture [USDA]. 2007. An assessment of fuel treatment effects on fire behavior, suppression effectiveness, and structure ignition on the Angora Fire. R5-TP-025. Manuscript on file at: U.S. Department of Agriculture, Forest Service, Pacfic Southwest Region, Valejo, CA.

U.S. Department of Agriculture [USDA]; U.S. Department of the Interior, Bureau of Land Management. 2007a. An assessment of fuel treatments on three large 2007 pacific northwest fires. Manuscript on file at: U.S. Department of Agriculture, Pacific Northwest Region, Portland, OR.

U.S. Department of Agriculture [USDA]. 2008. Fuel treatment effectiveness report: Gunbarrel Wildland Fire use. Manuscript on file at: U.S. Department of Agriculture, Forest Service, Shoshone National Forest, Cody WY.

U.S. Department of Agriculture [USDA], Forest Service. 2011. Fuel Treatment Effectiveness database. Unpublished data on file with: Paul Langowski, Branch Chief, Fuels and Fire Ecology, Rocky Mountain Region, U.S. Forest Service, 740 Simms Street, Golden, CO 80401-4702.

Response: *Where appropriate we added the suggested references.*

Colorado State Forest Service Comments

The Fourmile Canyon Fire, as an event, is important and relevant because it provides the opportunity to identify and discuss the what, where, when, how, and why the fire occurred and behaved the way it did. The elements that make the Fourmile Canyon Fire a subject of interest include the media (and therefore public) attention and awareness it drew, proximity to large population centers, how it spread relative to time and space, the number of homes threatened and destroyed, fire behavior influenced by fuels, weather, prior fuels treatment, and suppression response.

The foundation for discussion is based on factual information available prior to, during, and after the event. The Rocky Mountain Research Station was chartered to collect information about the Fourmile Canyon Fire and compile that information in a report.

The draft preliminary report was made available to the agencies having jurisdiction for their internal review with the request to look at the report with a critical eye on what the report missed (gaps) and areas that need clarification.

The Colorado State Forest Service distributed the draft preliminary report within the organization to Fire Program Managers, Fire Management Officers, Fire Behavior Analysts, and other personnel with experience in working with fire departments, counties, and landowners in all aspects of cooperative wildfire protection. Responses ranged from general observations of gaps in the preliminary draft to specific comments dealing with clarity or accuracy of data or information.

The reviewed and summarized responses follow.

General Comments:

- This report has the potential to be very valuable in stimulating discussion that will inform decision makers. The information (data) collected needs to be cited as what it is and what it is not. Any suggestion that the information in the report is all inclusive when it may only be what was available will diminish the credibility of the report. Any perception that the report attempts to influence rather than inform will diminish the credibility and value of the report as a tool to stimulate discussion.

Response: *The review is intended to present comprehensive factual information within the constraints of time and resources without policy and management judgments.*

- The recommendations and conclusions drawn by the contributors to the report are valuable but care should be taken to clearly describe the context in which they are submitted.

  Response: Only factual information is presented in this report. Recommendations are left to management.

- Context is always important. The Fourmile Canyon Fire occurred during a specific time frame under specific conditions and resulted in specific outcomes. It was not possible to reconstruct, identify, or collect information on all the variables that occurred during this dynamic wildfire event. Gaps in information need to be clearly recognized and clearly stated in the report.

  Response: Every effort was made in this report to present the limitations of the data along with the findings.

- There needs to be information in the report explaining how treatments occur on private lands and the constraints that influence those treatments, such as the voluntary nature (non-mandated) of treatments, non-contiguous parcels, small lot sizes, etc. Treating on public lands is a different situation than treating private lands and there needs to be some discussion on that so the reader has a clear understanding of the situation.

  Response: The landownership patterns are presented in the report. However, the objectives of this review were to report on the biophysical facts of the Fourmile Canyon Fire. These findings can then serve as a basis for later examination of the sociopolitical implications and management options.

- Prescriptions for USFS lands, typically larger acreages, are different than private land treatments, typically smaller acreages. Understanding the economies of scale at both the cost level and the objective of the treatment level is important.

  Response: Same comment as above.

Comments on Preliminary Report Areas:

Fuels Treatments:

- The report seems to stress or emphasize the negatives of fuels treatments. This perception may be due to examining the treatments in the context of stopping a fire from spreading or stopping a fire from burning homes. If so, this is a very narrow context. A broader context would be examining fuel treatments in how they influenced or affected fire behavior, safety, or some other objective. If the purpose of a treatment was to drop a fire out of the crowns or limit the potential of a surface fire from becoming a crown fire, then the treatment may be looked at as successful. If the purpose of a treatment was to increase sight distance along ingress and egress routes to improve safety, then the treatment may be looked at as successful. As with many silvicultural treatments, there are often multiple outcomes of a fuel treatment. The report should acknowledge that.

Response: This review was intended to objectively report factual information regarding fuel treatments along with the uncertainty surrounding any conclusions. As a scientific review, evaluation of fuel treatment performance with respect to the many objectives stated for treatments relied only on available evidence.

- Areas with fuel treatments are just a component of the entire fuel complex for this fire. Some discussion of the overall fuel conditions, including fuel treatments would be more representative of the overall conditions.

Response: The report contains descriptions of the fuel, topography, and weather conditions occurring across the entire landscape prior to the fire, including treatment conditions to the limits of available data.

- In the discussion on the efficacy of fuels treatment the report makes the statement "High winds and the low relative humidity of the air during the Fourmile Canyon Fire are common weather conditions associated with all large wildfires along the Front Range foothills and, thus, should be considered when developing prescriptions." This assumes that the purpose of fuel treatments is to protect values only during large fires; that fuel treatments exist that could protect values during extreme burning conditions. One of the assumptions made in the report is that the purpose of these mitigation efforts is to only protect these structures during extreme fire events and ignores the benefits from smaller scale fires that do not receive the political and media attention. Fire mitigation project design is a combination of a number of factors including fire behavior, economics, and societal values. Many home owners are not able or willing to make their homes "fire-proof" because of the financial or aesthetic sacrifices required.

- The analysis makes the assumption that all fuel treatments should be designed with absolute worst-case conditions in mind. It would be analogous to designing vehicle seat-belts and air-bags to protect the passengers from a free-fall off a cliff. It ignores fiscal and societal constraints.

Response: This section is located on page 63 of the Preliminary Findings. The sentence has been edited to broaden the performance metrics for fuel treatments. However, the Fourmile Canyon Fire occurred under extreme weather conditions that are climatologically common on the Front Range in Colorado, are common to the large fires that occur there, and are associated with the most damaging fires to both natural resources and developed values. Thus, the commonness of these fire conditions is not analogous to "free-fall off a cliff" but more appropriately to ordinary automobile accidents for which engineered safety measures are designed and proven to be effective. As noted in the report, fuel treatment prescriptions have been well documented as changing behavior even under extreme conditions. No assumptions are made that this is the sole purpose of treatments. The treatment prescriptions did not specify performance objectives related to weather or fire behavior and did not confer measurable benefits during the common fire conditions associated with the Fourmile Canyon Fire. The report contains no mention of "fireproof," which is an inappropriate expectation for performance. Research is noted in the Home Destruction section that indicates that effective reductions in home ignition potential is neither financially nor aesthetically severe.

Specific Comments:

- References to Colorado State Forestry should be: Colorado State Forest Service.

  Response: Corrected.

- Pages 4 and 5: The figures say "US Forest Service Boundaries" when "National Forest Boundaries" would be more correct.

  Response: Corrected.

- Page 20: The report discusses "Weather," "Winds," and "Fuel Treatments." Weather: The weather discussion actually is more climate related and has more bearing on fuel moistures than the weather. It discusses at length the Energy Release Component (ERC). While ERC is a good trend indicator it does not take into account actual fire potential because it excludes wind. The use of the NFDRS Spread Component (SC) and/or Burning Index (BI) give a better indication of fire potential for a given day due to the inclusion of the effects of wind.

  Response: Climate conveys the context for specific fire weather. Fuel moistures are closely related to ERC and the cumulative effect of months of weather patterns. ERC is known from research to be the best fire danger rating index precisely because it reflects fire occurrence potential rather than short-term fire behavior.

- Wind: The report discusses maximum wind gusts, but the average sustained wind speed is a more critical measure of the impacts of the winds. Wind gusts are an event, while sustained wind speed is a condition. The National Fire Danger Rating System uses an average 20 foot wind speed for calculations, not peak wind gusts.

  Response: The review team is very familiar with the National Fire Danger Rating System. Average winds are shown along with the gusts in Figure 28. The wind discussion was expanded, which includes a Burning Index trace. These additions will also account for the 10-minute average winds as well as the previous comment.

- Fuel Treatments: Areas with fuel treatments are just a component of the entire fuel complex for this fire. Some discussion of the overall fuel conditions, including fuel treatments would be more representative of the overall conditions.

  Response: Fuel conditions across the entire area are described along with the treatment conditions to within limits of available evidence.

- Many fire analysis's have their fire behavior sections grouped into "Climate," "Fuels," "Weather," and "Topography."

  Response: Information on all of these elements is presented in the report.

- Page 37: The report discusses how initial attention was given to evacuations and point protection. It concludes with "While responding units found this frustrating, it likely contributed to the overall safety of firefighters and the general public during the first day of the fire." This is a statement that is speculative and not supported by any data found in the report.

Response: This is not a speculative statement. We have reworked this section to clarify what was meant by this. This statement was in response to the staging of incoming resources by command staff during initial attack. This sometimes led to a delay in assigning suppression resources to the fire ground. A reference has been added that attributes this to the "Boulder County Type 3 Incident Management Team After Action Review."

- Page 38: This narrative concerning this graph concentrates on wind gusts and ignores sustained wind speeds. The sustained windspeeds at the time of the ignition were substantial and contributed to the fire behavior.

  Response: The report does not suggest that sustained 10-minute average windspeeds are irrelevant to fire behavior. The gust speed is known to better reflect the variability in winds and is more sensitive representation of temporal changes.

- Page 40: The report refers to "Nelson's dead fuel moisture meter using weather readings from the Sugarloaf RAWS (Nelson 2000)" yet the cited documentation in the references is "Prediction of diurnal change in 10-h fuel stick moisture content" by Ralph M. Nelson, Jr." There is no discussion in that article about a meter that can be used to estimate 1-hour fuel moisture. The fixation with peak wind gusts continues on this page.

  Response: Typographical error "meter" is now corrected to model. Reference to wind gusts has been addressed in previous comments. Additional citation from Oklahoma Mesonet studies expanding the Nelson model to additional fuel size classes is included.

- Page 67: Figure 46 shows pictures of a house where "low burn severity" is attributed to "treatment of the surface fuels and canopy." This house is owned by Dave Steinmann, who is a volunteer on the Gold Hill VFD. Dave never evacuated, but stayed at his house as the fire came up out of Fourmile Canyon towards Gold Hill. He has an "Intelliguard" foam system powered by compressed nitrogen, which he used as the fire approached to foam down his house, as well as the surrounding vegetation. He was quite proud of the system, it's in the shed attached to the side of the house. His actions during the fire likely saved the house (along with his fuel treatments). The important point here is that this house is probably not the best example of fuel treatment effects on fire behavior, since the fuels were actually foamed by the landowner as the fire approached.

  Response: The report states that Mr. Steinmann's claims of surface fuel removal and the apparent low severity on his property are consistent with what is known about the effectiveness of surface fuel treatment in moderating fire behavior. Caption on photo 46 has been edited to only reference vegetation. Interview with Mr. Steinmann contradicts the statement that vegetation was treated with foam. He actually used his weed-eater as the fire approached to further reduce the amount and continuity of surface fuels.

- Page 78: There is a significant amount of discussion concerning the survival of structures in the fire perimeter and effect of defensible space in the "home ignition zone." The report makes the interesting observation "we found home survival within

USDA Forest Service Gen. Tech. Rep. RMRS-GTR-289. 2012

105

areas of destruction, destruction within areas of survival and homes destroyed surrounded by unconsumed, green vegetation." Missing is any detailed discussion or analysis on the effect of differing building materials on the survival of structures.

Response: Additional explanation has been included in the text to address why no interpretation can be made concerning effect of building materials on structure survival or building damage.

- Page 88-90: The following statements are made in the summary: "Gusty winds, not unusual along the Front Range, were consistently blowing at 35 mph with gusts greater than 40 mph." yet the data provided on page 38 indicates a lower consistent wind speed.

Response: Wording has been revised to be consistent with Figure 28.

- "Only fires that burn under extreme weather, e.g., high winds, low air relative humidity, and burn dry fuels escape initial attack." There was no data cited for such a conclusion.

Response: Wording has been revised.

- "At ignition the fine dead fuels (grasses, needles etc.) had a moisture content of 5%. At ignition the probability of these fuels igniting was 55% and by 17:00 the probability of ignition was 90%." These statements are jumbled and the term "probability of ignition" is used out of the correct context in this situation.

Response: Probability of ignition was correctly calculated.

- "High winds and low air humidity during the Fourmile Canyon Fire are common weather conditions associated with all large wildfires along the Front Range and, thus, should be accounted for in any fuel treatment prescription." The analysis makes the assumption that all fuel treatments should be designed with absolute worst-case conditions in mind. It would be analogous to designing vehicle seatbelts and air-bags to protect the passengers from a free-fall off a cliff. It ignores fiscal and societal constraints.

Response: This comment has been addressed – see previous response.

Bureau Land Management Comments

After reviewing the Fourmile Canyon Fire Preliminary Findings, BLM Colorado has the following recommendations.

- Clarify Fuels Projects: Currently, the document (page 27) states that the Colorado State Forest Service (CSFS) administered 417 acres of fuels treatments within the final fire perimeter. The BLM would like to clarify the fact that 113 acres of those fuels treatments were on BLM lands, and were administered by the CSFS using the Good Neighbor Authority. Through the Good Neighbor Authority, the BLM transferred $94,000 to the CSFS for fuels reduction projects on BLM-managed lands in areas where the CSFS was assisting with projects on private lands within Boulder County.

Response: The report was revised to clarify land ownership and acreage.

- Efficiency of Fuels Treatments: Currently, the document reads as if all treatments were ineffective. The BLM feels that the effectiveness of treatments in the Fourmile Canyon Fire area was variable and served different purposes. For instance, Dave Steinman's house (figure 46) was part of a larger fuels project that may have contributed to decreased fire severity at the upper end of Emerson Gulch. The document points out that this area is an example of a homeowner treating both canopy and surface fuels; however, this is part of a larger treatment that may have helped the area to the north of Dixon Road. It was part of one treatment, not just one landowner's treatment. Another example is Boulder County's Bald Mountain project where the restoration project may have aided in stopping the fire progression as the fire was out of the tree canopies and in grass at this point. In addition, there is some evidence to suggest that some of the treatment areas were used during suppression activities, particularly around Lee Hill. The Boulder Mountain Fire Protection District used the thinnings in this area to gain access to the fire perimeter and aid in suppression. The combination of treated acres and the use of aerial retardant contributed to the success of suppression efforts in that area (please contact Steve Lynn for additional information, 303-440-0235).

Response: The burn severity around Mr. Steinmann's home was referenced only in regards to the claim of additional surface fuel manipulation, which was consistent with research conclusions regarding the importance of surface fuel reduction to fuel treatment effects. While the review recognizes the larger extent of fuel treatment along Dixon Road, Figure 47 revealed high burn severity and canopy consumption in the entire unit except near Mr. Steinmann's property. As with many treatments, changes in burn severity related to this treatment location are confounded by slope and aspect changes (change to north facing slope) and accompanying microclimate and wind effects. In other words, live canopy was evident in areas on the northern slope even in the absence of adjacent treatment.

Regarding the Bald Mountain fuel treatments, we don't see any evidence of fire behavior modification by fuel treatment here. The map on Figure 45 shows that only 2.5 acres of fuel treatment burned (canopy consumed). The fire spread beyond the treatment into the open grassland. The majority of the Bald Mountain treatment unit was south of the main fire edge and not burned.

Regarding fuel treatment uses for suppression near Lee Hill, this is referred to as the Church Camp fuels treatment unit. We are aware of claims made regarding impressions of increased safety by hand crews building line. We did not include this in the report, because (1) the line was constructed on September 8th, during a period of little fire spread activity, and (2) as detailed on page 51, the Unit Log for Division "G" recorded that on September 7th between the hours of 1300 to 1700 active burning in the same area lead to a strike-team of engines to disengage and retreat to Boulder Heights Fire Station Number 2 (revealing concern for firefighter safety not mitigated by the presence of nearby fuel treatment). Retardant was used along the entire east flank of the fire on September 7th in areas with and without treatment. With the moderation of the weather, the treatment was not reached by the fire; the effectiveness of retardant drops cannot be determined, with or without a contribution by treatment.

- Update Costs to Date: According to the BLM's accounting system (Financial and Business Management System), the cost to the BLM for its efforts relative to the Fourmile fire as of August 19, 2011, was $1,479,150.58. It appears that the cost share amounts for participating agencies are not congruent (pages 80 and 83). The document states that the share is based off land mass equal to 22.6 percent; however, later cites 28 percent as the cost share. The report should also explain why the United States Forest Service is the responsible entity for aviation, and clarify how the Federal Fire and Aviation financial organization operates.

Response: *We were able to distinguish among agency funding of suppression; however, post fire rehabilitation costs were not as clear so we chose to report total federal costs not by specific agency. We have added discussion of BLM BAER costs to the report.*

BLM Colorado would also like you to consider the following suggestions, which speak to the socioeconomic and human factors that can sway our ability as land managers to prevent future devastation by wildfire.

- Land Ownership in Relation to Fuels Treatments: The document should address how land ownership patterns and topography impact fuels treatment decisions and designs. Because most of the fuels work in this area was on private land, coordination and project support was critical (more than 600 landowners existed within the fire perimeter). Oftentimes, social attitudes, budgets and topography compromise our ability to develop and implement effective hazardous fuels treatment projects.

  Response: *Land ownership was presented in the report. This is not a management or policy review. The objectives of this review were to document the biophysical facts related, in part, to fuel treatments (among others). These facts can inform subsequent management discussions of the opportunities and constraints facing fuel management in the future.*

- Prescription of Performance: The revisions of the "prescription of performance" within the document should speak to criteria used for thinning standards, mastication standards and prescribed fire needs or feasibility and if those objectives were met. The document does not address specific treatment objectives. If these specific objectives were available, then they should be included in the report. If not, the report should recommend specific treatment objectives for future mechanical and prescribed fire treatments.

  Response: *We did not have enough information on treatment activities to evaluate compliance with contract standards. Standards are not equivalent to objectives or necessarily related to performance under wildfire conditions relative to those objectives. We did not find evidence of objectives for the treatments relative to fire behavior, burn severity, fire movement, suppression assistance, or weather conditions (see page 34).*

- Prescribed Fire: Fire is a very natural occurrence in the Ponderosa ecosystem, as well as the geographic area that the Fourmile fire and other larger incidents have occurred. The report should address the benefits and drawbacks to using prescribed fire, and how it could have played a role in the Fourmile area. Given the existing evidence to support the uses of prescribed treatments and its role in reducing fuels and fire intensity, there is an opportunity here to show readers where prescribed treatments can be successful. More often than not, fear or concerns over escaped prescribed fire and smoke and/or air quality limits our ability to plan and implement safe and well-executed treatments.

Response: *Benefits of prescribed fire for fuel treatment are discussed and references cited. Specific objectives and challenges are particular to each locality and it is beyond the scope of this report to describe all that may apply.*

- Removal of Activity Fuels: The report should address whether or not it is acceptable to haul away fuels to allocated dumpsites or eliminate masticated activity fuels. The report should also address whether or not the 417 acres of completed hazard fuels treatments were actually effective in relationship to total acres burned in the fire. In reality, can a fuels treatment truly be developed to prevent destruction given expected low relative humidity, high winds, extreme topography, and geographic drought?

Response: *The intent of this report is to document the biophysical facts associated with the Fourmile Canyon Fire. The range of possible options for disposing of masticated fuels is beyond the scope of this report. The evidence available on fuel treatment performance was assessed in the report. Questions concerning how much fuel treatment is required to achieve various objectives are beyond the scope of this report.*

USDA Forest Service Gen. Tech. Rep. RMRS-GTR-289. 2012

109

Appendix C: Summary of Contacted Individuals _____

Bureau of Land Management	10
U.S. Geological Survey	3
Boulder County	14
U.S. Forest Service	13
Fire Departments/Protection Districts	12
Private citizens	2
National Park Service	3
Colorado State Forest Service	7
National Oceanic and Atmospheric Administration	1
Geographic Area Coordination Center	1
News/photographers	5
Other	6
Total	77